アメリカ人の本音
THE TRUTH ABOUT AMERICANS

マックス・フォン・シュラー 著
Max von Schuler

Both English and Japanese texts are written by the author.
本文は英語・日本語共に著者の執筆に依る。

For America in the near future, Japanese goodwill and cooperation will be essential for America. And I have to say, Americans should make more effort to keep that goodwill. And then both countries shall be able to face the future together, in partnership.

アメリカの将来の為には、日本との親善と協力は不可欠です。そして、日本との親善を守る為に、アメリカ人は日本人の理解にもっと努めるべきです。そうしてこそ、両国は真の友人となって21世紀の世界をリードすることができるでしょう。

～ Max von Schuler

CONTENTS 目次

PROLOGUE A STORY FROM THE BLACK SHIPS
序章　黒船の論　　　　　　　　　　　　　　　　9

CHAPTER 1 JAPAN, 161 YEARS IN THE SHADOW OF THE BLACK SHIPS
第1章　黒船の陰に有る161年間の日米関係　　　15

Arrival of the Matthew Perry squadron ペリー来航	16
American exceptionalism アメリカ例外主義	18
Philosophy of Japan 日本の哲学	20
War and Peace 戦争と平和	23
American lies アメリカ人の嘘	28
Illusion of Globalization 国際化の幻想	33
Geisha and sex 芸者とセックス	36
Uneducated Americans 教養のないアメリカ人	41
Fear of Japan 日本に対する恐れ	43
Immigrants and society 移民と社会	47
TPP - American way of doing business TPP-アメリカ式ビジネスのやり方	49

The Emperor and the Imperial Household 天皇と皇室	52
Japan-Korea dispute 日韓問題	54
Korea was not a colony of Japan 朝鮮は日本の植民地ではなかった	56

CHAPTER 2   THE ROAD TO WAR, DREAMS OF CHINA
第2章　戦争への道、中国に対する夢　　63

Russo-Japanese War and rise of Japan 日露戦争と日本の台頭	64
Immigrants and discrimination 移民と差別	65
Christianity and superiority キリスト教と優位性	73
Demonization of Japan 日本の悪魔化イメージ作り	77
Conquering the Philippines フィリピン征服	83
Two reasons for the Japan-U.S. war 日米戦争の2つの理由	85
Three Americans in charge 3人のアメリカ人戦争責任者	92
Interventionist Americans 干渉するアメリカ人	96
China, an invading nation 侵略する中国	100
8 point plan to force Japan to start a war 日本に戦争を始めさせる8つの計画	105
Was there a way to prevent the war? 戦争を避ける方法はありましたか？	109

Japanese spirit was the core of
    the post war prosperity and power　　112
日本精神が戦後の日本の繁栄と力の中心に
Korea uses the United States　　115
アメリカを利用する韓国

CHAPTER 3　THE PACIFIC WAR
第3章　大東亜戦争　　119

The truth about the Japanese military　　120
日本帝国陸海軍の真実

Nanking Incident　　128
南京事件

The firebombing of Japan　　134
日本の空襲

Fear of the Christian Fundamentalists　　138
キリスト教原理主義の恐怖

Comfort Women (Camp Followers)　　140
軍人相手の売春婦

American feminists and Korean activists　　146
アメリカのフェミニストと韓国活動家

The Contradiction of U.S. military　　149
アメリカ軍の矛盾

An example of a debate　　152
ディベートレクチャー

The Tokubetsukogekitai　　156
特別攻撃隊

Japan, the first nation that declared racial equality　　174
人種の平等を最初に謳った日本

CHAPTER 4   AFTER THE WAR
第 4 章　戦後 179

Masochistic Japanese 180
マゾヒスティック（自虐的）日本人

About Yasukuni Shrine 190
靖国神社について

A letter to America 195
アメリカへの手紙

Things to learn from Japanese people 203
日本人から学ぶこと

A letter to Korea 209
韓国への手紙

A note to China 218
中国へのノート

Japan and the future 220
日本と将来

To sum it up 223
最後に

EPILOGUE
終わりに 229

参考文献 236

序章　黒船の論

Prologue　A story from the Black Ships

Prologue A story from the Black Ships

By chance, I was watching a TV show the other night. It was about the difficulties Japanese have in learning English. I really felt discomforted watching the show. The underlining theme was that English is some master language, and all Japanese must strive to learn it.

This kind of idea is very harmful to Japan, particularly in dealings with foreigners, and especially with Americans.

少し前にたまたま見たテレビ番組で、日本人が英語を学ぶ難しさについて、取り上げていました。その番組を見て何となく変な気持ちになりました。基本的なテーマは、英語は偉い言葉で、全ての日本人が英語を勉強する必要がある、ということでしたので。

このような考え方は、日本に有害です。外国人と取引をする際、特に、アメリカ人、向こうの文化が偉いという考えが日本に有害になります。

There was a foreigner who commonly appears on television, correcting some Japanese person's pronunciation of choux creme. He said it sounded like shoe cream. Well first of all, the proper English word is shoe polish, shoe cream is rather obscure.

There was another person who used wooden chopsticks to form people's tongues into the proper position to pronounce English correctly.

And Choux creme pastry is French, I have never seen it in America. It was a ridiculous sequence in the show. There is some kind of masochistic feeling towards America in modern Japanese culture. And this hurts Japanese people in business and everyday life when dealing with America.

またあるテレビでよく出る外国人が、日本人の〝シュークリーム〟の発音を直していました。靴磨き用の〝シュークリーム〟み

たいな発音だと言いました。しかし、私は英語でシュークリームという言葉を聞いた事が無く、非常に珍しいです。正しくは〝シューポリッシュ〟です。

　もう一人の人は割り箸を利用して、人の舌の形を正しい英語の発音が出来る様に直していました。

　それと、シュークリーム はフランスのお菓子で、私はアメリカで見た事がありません。それはその番組の変なコーナーでした。現在の日本人の心の中で、アメリカに対して何かマゾヒスチックな気持ちがあるみたいです。このマゾヒスチックな日本人の態度は、アメリカ人とのビジネスや日常生活における交渉の時にとても困ります。

But I am not writing a book on how to learn English. There are very many such books. My goal is to help Japanese people understand how to deal with Americans, and how Americans think. And I will go the other way. I also want to explain to Americans that Japan is not an evil nation.

That is correct, Americans have a very vague understanding of The Pacific War. They basically believe that Japan was an evil dictatorship until America defeated Japan in WWII, and gave Japan democracy. And Americans believe that all Japanese secretly desire to be Americans. Not true at all.

　しかし、私は英語の習い方の本を書くつもりはありません。そういう本は数多く有ります。私の目標は、日本人の皆さんに、アメリカ人との付き合い方や対処する方法、アメリカ人の考え方を説明したいと考えます。それからもう一つ、反対向きに、アメリカ人に、日本は悪の国では無いということを教えたいと考えます。

　だってアメリカ人は大東亜戦争の真実をあまり分かっていませんし、基本的に、アメリカ人の考えでは、戦前の日本は悪の独裁国家で、敗戦後アメリカが日本に民主主義を教え、与えたと考え

Prologue A story from the Black Ships

ているからです。そしてアメリカ人は、日本人全員が心の中ではアメリカ人になりたいと思っている、と信じています。全然違います。

So how to communicate with Americans? You have to start from a strong position. You state your positive points. Too many Japanese people have too strong a sense of deference towards Americans.

それでは、アメリカ人とどう話したら良いでしょうか？ まず、強い立場から始めたら良いです。自分の肯定的な点を言います。アメリカ人に対して、強い敬意や服従の気持ちを持っている日本人が多過ぎです。

In recent negotiations about TPP, Japanese negotiators seem to lose every point. Some of my Japanese friends say to me, "But America is a good country, they would not do anything bad." Well, America is not an evil country of course. But America does very strongly move for it's own profit, and if that hurts Japan, well too bad.

In Japanese culture, various different companies in the same field can cooperate. For example in the Auto industry. One company might reduce it's sales for a time to help other companies in the industry. Americans cannot understand this. Cooperation between different companies is rare in America, each company tries to get as much profit for itself as it can. Americans think of business like war.

最近のTPP交渉でも、日本チームはすべてのポイントで負けているみたいです。何人かの日本人の友人が、「アメリカは悪い事をしないでしょう」と言います。まあ、勿論、アメリカは悪い国

ではないですが、必ず自国の国益の為に動きます。その結果日本人が困ったとしても、全然気にしません。

　日本の文化では、同じ業界における様々な会社がお互いの為に協力をすることが出来ます。例えば、自動車産業です。他の会社を助ける為に、ある会社は一時的に売り上げを下げるかも知れません。アメリカ人はこのような行為を理解出来ません。会社同士の協力はアメリカでは珍しいことで、どんな会社でも自分の利益が第一だからです。アメリカ人の感覚では、ビジネスと戦争は同じ事なのです。

　And not just how to understand Americans. In recent years Japan is having difficulties with China and South Korea. It seems that all those two countries can cry out is "History, history, history!" Well, I will write about that history in this book. And I will also write why some people need to keep bashing Japan with the history problem.

　I will comment on Japan's change from the Edo era through the Meiji period. And also, I will write a lot about WWII. Too many Americans still don't understand that the war in Europe and the war in the Pacific were two different wars.

　それから、アメリカ人を理解する方法だけを書くつもりはありません。最近、日本は中国と韓国との間に問題があります。その二つの国は、いつでも〝歴史！歴史！歴史！〟と叫んでいるみたいですね。そこで、その歴史についてもこの本に書きます。それと、何故その国がいつも日本に歴史問題で攻撃するのか、その理由も書きます。

　また、江戸時代から明治時代の日本の近代国家化について書きます。勿論、大東亜戦争の事も書きます。現在でも、ヨーロッパの第二次世界大戦と大東亜戦争は全然違うという真実を分かっていないアメリカ人が多過ぎるのです。

Prologue A story from the Black Ships

And for the Koreans: During the war you were enthusiastically Japanese, now you are enthusiastically victims. It is very strange.

韓国人に一言：大東亜戦争では、貴方達は熱狂的に日本人として戦いましたが、戦後から熱狂的に犠牲者です。変ですね。

I am an immigrant in Japan. My grandfather was born in Sweden, and emigrated to America. So I think I can compare the two experiences. And in this book I will. It is much easier to come to Japan rather than America. Japan is a unique country in this world. It is time for Japan to stand up and be proud of itself. I have had many fantastic experiences in Japan, and am proud to be an immigrant in this country.

私は日本への移民です。私の祖父はスウェーデンに生まれて、アメリカへ移民しました。この二つの経験をこの本で比較します。アメリカに移民するより、日本へ移民する方が全然しやすいということをご存じですか。日本は世界の中でも珍しい国です。日本人は誇りを持つべきです。私は日本でいっぱい素晴らしい経験がありますし、日本に移民する事について誇りがあります。

I will now introduce the the truth about Americans that people in Japan do not know.

私の日本での経験と日本の皆さんが知らない、本当のアメリカ人の本音をここに紹介します。

第 1 章　黒船の陰に有る 161 年間の日米関係

Chapter 1　Japan, 161 years in the shadow of the Black Ships

Chapter 1 Japan, 161 years in the shadow of the Black Ships

Arrival of the Matthew Perry squadron
ペリー来航

This year, it is fully 161 years since Commodore Perry forced his way into Japan, and caused Japan to open it's borders to the world. I lived here in Japan for 40 of those years. That is really 1/4 of the time that Japan and America have had relations. Since I was born in America and spent my early years there, I think that I can comment on that relationship.

One of the first things that I think of are that Americans are not very different in attitude than Commodore Perry and people of his age. Americans are always filled with themselves. They approach every problem or situation thinking that America is the most essential country in the world.

How the Japanese viewed the Black Ships
日本人が見た黒船の姿です
出典：『黒船の図』／無款
Massachusetts Institute of Technology Black Ships & Samurai

16

第 1 章　黒船の陰に有る 161 年間の日米関係

　今年でペリー提督が江戸時代の鎖国政策を強制的に開国に向かわせてから 161 年になります。私は今まで 40 年間日本に住んできましたが、それは、日米関係の 4 分の 1 と同じ期間です。私はアメリカで生まれ育ったので、この日米関係について、面白い話が出来ると思います。
　まず最初に思うことは、その当時のアメリカ人と現在のアメリカ人の態度はほとんど同じだということです。アメリカ人はいつも自分の事を中心に考え、どんな問題でも解決する為には、アメリカが絶対に必要であると思っています。

Commodore Perry felt that he had a mission from God. It was his duty to force Japan to become Christian, and to do business with America. No, Commodore Perry did not evangelize Japan himself, but he provided the opportunity for American missionaries to come to Japan. Japan's feelings on the subject of relations with Western countries played no part in Commodore Perry's deliberations.

　ペリー提督は自分は神様から使命を受けていると信じていました。日本を強制的にキリスト教へ改宗させ、アメリカと商取引をさせるのは自分の義務であると思っていました。ペリー提督は自分自身福音を説く事はしませんでしたが、アメリカの宣教師が来日する機会を作りました。日本の江戸幕府が西洋国との交流についてどう思うかということは、ペリー提督の計画には全く関係有りませんでした。

During my life in Japan, I have met many foreigners here, mainly part time English teachers and part time actors. Frankly, I was always astounded at the arrogance of these people. They felt that by being English teachers in Japan, they were fulfilling some essential role, without which Japan would collapse. And their behavior was almost always rude.

The first foreigners who came here also behaved rudely and badly. They had no respect for Japanese culture and customs. And they did not learn to speak Japanese. Until very recently, few Americans living in Japan learned to speak Japanese. I will now explain how Americans think.

私は日本に住んでいて、多くの外国人と会った事がありますが、ほとんどは英語の先生、パートタイムのテレビタレントでした。正直に言うと、この人たちの傲慢にいつも驚きました。彼らの考えでは、ただの在日英語教師なのに、自分たちはものすごく大切な活動をしている、自分たちが居ないと日本が崩壊する、と考えていました。そして、いつも本当に失礼で無礼でした。

明治時代の初めに来た外国人も、ほとんどは失礼で、無礼な態度でした。日本の文化と習慣に対して尊敬が有りませんでした。勿論、日本語を覚えませんでした。最近まで、日本語が出来るアメリカ人の数は本当に少なかったです。このアメリカ人の考えを私は皆さんに解説していきます。

American exceptionalism
アメリカ例外主義

There is a certain philosophy in America, which can be called American exceptionalism. Basically, it is the belief that America is the most superior nation on Earth. And that God has given America the right to dominate all nations on Earth.

And to convert them to American Protestant Christianity. Whether they want to or not. That is why Commodore Perry referred to his mission as "God given". And it is why in general

Americans are so poor at other languages.　Why should an American learn another language, or about another culture, when American English and culture are the greatest on Earth?

　アメリカにはある哲学があります。それは「アメリカ例外主義」と言います。基本的に、この信念はアメリカは世界で一番上位の国である、ということ、そして、アメリカは神様から世界の国々を支配する使命を受けている、ということです。

　それから、アメリカ型のキリスト教プロテスタントに、強制的に改宗させる事も神様からの使命であると考えています。相手国がキリスト教へ改宗する希望が有っても無くても強制的に行ないます。その哲学から、ペリー提督は自分のこの使命を「神様から与えられた」と言っていたのです。一般的に、アメリカ人は他国の言語が出来ないのはそのためです。自分の国が世界で一番素晴らしいのに、どうして他国の文化、言葉を勉強する必要があるのか？という考えがあるからです。

　Basically, this idea has not changed since the time of Commodore Perry.　"America has a mission from God to dominate the world, and other countries should thank America for this.　This is what most Americans believe.　For Japanese, Americans are easy to understand, because they voice their opinions strongly.

　基本的な考えはペリー提督の時代と変わっていません。「アメリカは神様から世界を支配する特別な使命を与えられている、それは相手の国にとっても喜ばれるのは当然である」です。ほとんどのアメリカ人がこれを信じています。日本人がアメリカ人と付き合う時は、相手は本気でそう信じて疑わない人達と思えば、随分と理解がしやすいでしょう。

Chapter 1 Japan, 161 years in the shadow of the Black Ships

Philosophy of Japan
日本の哲学

The gifts Commodore Perry presented to Japan by America, and to America by Japan, show interesting aspects of each others national character.

America was then, and still is, a very new nation. Americans take much pride in their technology. Among the American presents were: A large quantity of various types of alcohol, guns and swords, a working train and track, a telegraph set. Japan presented America with many works of art, such as lacquerware. The Americans could understand the fine craftsmanship that went into producing such Japanese art works, but decided that they had no commercial value.

　ペリー提督が日本に渡した贈り物と、日本がアメリカに渡した贈り物で両国の哲学の違いが分かります。
　アメリカは当時も現在も、新しい国です。アメリカ人は自分達のテクノロジーに誇りを持っています。アメリカから日本への贈り物は、洋酒の色々な種類、銃と刀、蒸気機関車と線路、電報通信セットでした。日本からアメリカへの贈り物は、芸術品、例えば、漆器でした。アメリカ人はその日本の職人の技術力を認めましたが、日本の物は商品としては価値が無いと判断しました。

And Japanese cuisine did not impress the Americans at all. In the diary of chief interpreter Williams, he estimated that the banquet had little monetary value. The Americans did think that Japanese service at the banquet was extremely polite. But the Americans thought the food they had been served in Okinawa previously much better, since it consisted of many pork dishes.

　ペリー提督と一緒に来たアメリカ人達は、日本料理には全く良い印象を持ちませんでした。通訳のウィリアムズの日記には、日本幕府が出した宴会の料理は経済的にみて価値が低いものである、と書いてあったのです。しかし、日本のサービスはとても丁寧であるとも思っていました。ペリー提督の黒船の艦隊は東京湾へ来る前に沖縄を訪問したので、黒船の乗組員は沖縄料理の方が良かったと思っていました。それは何故かというと、豚肉料理が多かったからです。

About 15 years ago or so, I played Commodore Perry in an NHK recreation drama. In the scene the entire banquet served to Commodore Perry was recreated, and I was amazed! It was fantastic and luxurious. Well, I have lived in Japan for 40 years, and I deeply appreciate Japanese food. In particular, I am fascinated by the fruit Yuzu. You simply do not bite into it like an orange. Yet a few slices of yuzu peel and it transforms a dish. To understand and appreciate Japanese food, you have to look deeply into it.

　15年前位、私はNHKの再現ドラマでペリー提督の役をやり、そのシーンで、ペリー提督へ出された宴会料理を完全に再現したものが出されて、私は本当に驚きました。何と言ったらいいのか、とても素晴らしい料理でした！　私は日本に40年住んでいますので、日本料理の真価を本当に認めています。特に私は柚子が大好きです。オレンジのようにそのまま食べません！　柚子の皮をちょっと入れると、料理の味が変わります。日本料理を理解する為に、この繊細な部分を深く考える必要があります。

Chapter 1 Japan, 161 years in the shadow of the Black Ships

Obviously, Commodore Perry and his party preferred the American style of food, which is basically huge chunks of meat, accompanied by a mountain of vegetables. And the same is true today. A couple of years ago a friend of mine visited me in Japan. His first announcement to me was that he could absolutely not eat seafood. Well, considering that Japan is an island nation, that limited our choices considerably.

But he simply had no interest in trying new things, which is true of most Americans. For most Americans, it is impossible to understand Japanese feelings. If they could, they could work well with Japanese people. It is simply impossible for most to comprehend this concept of Japanese thought.

　明らかに、ペリー提督と黒船の乗組員はアメリカでよく食べられている、厚切りの肉と山盛りの野菜、という様な料理を好んでいました。現在のアメリカ人も同じです。数年前に、アメリカの友達が私に会いに来日しました。最初の言葉は「私は海で取れた物は食べられません」。そんなことを言っても、日本は島国ですから、日本食を食べるのにその選択には限りがあります。

　しかし、彼はほとんどのアメリカ人に当てはまる感覚で、アメリカ食とは違う、新しいものを食べたいという気持ちは全く有りませんでした。多くのアメリカ人は日本人のような繊細な感性は理解できません。しかし、逆に言うとそれが理解できれば相手を満足させることは簡単です。繊細な含みのある言い方をして、それが日本の哲学であると言っても何を言っているか理解されません。

War and Peace
戦争と平和

There is another comparison between Americans and Japanese that I would like to mention here. Before the Meiji Restoration, for more than 260 years, Japan had been governed by a military government, the Tokugawa Bakufu. However, that military government never conducted even one war. Of course, all in all Japan has some 2,700 years or so of history, over which time Japanese culture was gradually built up.

　ここで、もう一つ日本とアメリカを比較したい事があります。明治維新までに、日本は260年以上の間、軍政府、徳川幕府が治めていました。しかし、その軍政府は一つの戦争もしていません。日本の歴史は2700年近くに及び、この長い時間をかけて日本の文化は少しずつ構築されてきたものです。

Today as I write this, America's own history is shorter than the Tokugawa Bakufu, yet there is almost no time in American history that a war was not being fought somewhere by Americans. American history is drenched in blood. During the Tokugawa Bakufu, the Japanese warrior class of Samurai evolved fighting techniques like archery into the art of Kyudo, or sword fighting into the art and sport of Kendo. But they did not fight wars, they valued peace.

　私がこの本を書いている今、アメリカの歴史は徳川幕府より短いにも関わらず、アメリカの歴史で戦争が無い時はほとんど有りませんでした。アメリカの歴史は血を流し続けびしょぬれです。徳川幕府の武士は、弓の武器としての使い方を弓道に、刀で戦う

Chapter 1 Japan, 161 years in the shadow of the Black Ships

戦い方を剣道に進化させました。戦う方法や道具が日本では芸術になりました。しかし、日本の江戸時代の武士は戦争をせず、平和を大切にしていました。

But America has nearly almost always been at war with somebody since it's foundation. I once used to think that the period from the end of the American Civil war in 1865 to the Spanish American war in 1898 was a period of peace. I had thought that the Great Slaughter of the American Civil war had shocked Americans, that they were tired of conflict.

But I forgot the Indian wars out West. These were wars of genocide. American troops made a point to kill women and children. The last battle of the Indian wars was at Wounded Knee in 1890. So this brings us to 8 years before war with Spain and the beginning of the American Empire. And that acquisition of the Philippines was a major cause of war with Japan.

しかし、アメリカは、建国してからいつも誰かと戦争をしてい

The American Civil War
アメリカの南北戦争です
出典：Library of Congress (Kurz & Allison, Art Publishers, 1891)

24

ます。1865年の南北戦争から1898年の米西戦争までの33年間は平和な時があり、その期間は南北戦争の大虐殺のショックでアメリカ人が戦争にうんざりしていたのだと昔は思っていました。

　しかしそうではなかったのです。私はアメリカ西部のインディアン戦争を忘れていました。この戦争は計画的な大虐殺で、アメリカ兵は躊躇なくインディアンの女性と子供を殺し、その最後の戦いは、1890年のウンデット・ニーの虐殺でした。これは、米西戦争とアメリカ帝国の始まりの8年前になります。そして、その後の、アメリカのフィリピン獲得は大東亜戦争の大きな原因となりました。

In any case, it is Americans who have always thought of Japanese people as being blood thirsty. All those images of Samurai, and Seppuku. The concept of Seppuku, or suicide for reasons of honor is something that Americans completely cannot understand.

　とにかく、アメリカ人はいつも日本人が血に飢えた残忍な民族だと思っています。単純に侍と切腹というイメージです。しかし、アメリカ人は切腹、つまり名誉の為という理由で自殺をする、そのコンセプトを全く理解出来ないと思います。

But American and Japanese wars were very different. Until the Meiji era, all Japanese wars were internal. The only one exception to this was Toyotomi Hideyoshi's two invasions of Korea. And those invasions eventually failed. American wars in general were wars of expansion and extermination. In fact, in America's expansion westward and across the Pacific was very violent. And Perry's visit to Japan came very close to becoming a war.

　しかしながら、日本とアメリカの戦争は全然違います。明治維新まで、日本の戦争はすべて国内でした。この例外は、豊臣秀吉

Chapter 1 Japan, 161 years in the shadow of the Black Ships

氏の二つの朝鮮侵略だけですし、その侵略は最終的に失敗しました。基本的に、アメリカの戦争は拡大の為で、それとその現地人を根絶する為でした。アメリカの西部侵攻と太平洋侵攻は本当に暴力的なものでした。そして、ペリー提督の訪問は宣戦布告に近いものでした。

There is another great difference between the Japanese and American ways of war. Japanese civil wars were between rival Daimyo's. They were not directed against civilians. Just take a look at typical Japanese castle.

The only people that would be protected inside the castle would be the warriors of the Daimyo and their families. The regular townspeople would be outside the castle during the battle. If the Daimyo in the castle lost, he simply was replaced by the winning Daimyo. And the townspeople would of course accept him as their new ruler.

In Europe, and in China and Korea, walls were built around the entire town. If the defenders lost, the townspeople were slaughtered along with the defeated soldiers.

アメリカ人と日本人の戦争のやり方には、もう一つ大きな違いが有ります。日本の内乱は大名同士で戦い、今で言う一般人を狙うことは有りませんでした。日本の典型的なお城を考えましょう。

お城の中で守備についている人は、大名の家臣である武士とその家族であり、町人は戦の間、お城の外にいます。もしお城の大名が負けた場合、その城主は勝った大名に取って代わられますが、それを町人は新しい支配者として受け入れます。

ヨーロッパ、中国、朝鮮では街の周りに塀を造りました。もし守備している兵が負けた場合、町人も負けた兵と一緒に虐殺されました。

第 1 章　黒船の陰に有る 161 年間の日米関係

The idea that Japanese are an aggressive and cruel people is simply not true. If we look at history, we find that it is America that is the violent country. Even now, America is involved in a war somewhere in the world. By looking at the history, we can tell that Japan is one of the most peaceful countries in the world.

　日本人が攻撃的だとか残忍だというのは嘘です。それはアメリカ人の方であることが歴史で証明されています。今でもそうですがアメリカは常にどこかで戦闘をしています。日本が一番平和的な民族であることは歴史を見れば明らかです。

Japanese castle
日本のお城です
出典：姫路城空撮（天守群）　姫路市役所

Chapter 1 Japan, 161 years in the shadow of the Black Ships

American lies
アメリカ人の嘘

The average Japanese person is very honest. Of course, there are crooked officials in Japan, but compared to other countries, Japanese are truly honest. And Japanese people easily believe other people. Very unfortunately, that is not true of Americans. This was true in Commodore Perry's time, and it is still true today.

　平均的に日本人は誠実、正直です。勿論、腐敗している官僚、政治家も居るけれど、他国と比較すると、日本人は本当に誠実、正直だと思います。日本人は素直に他人を信じますが、残念ながら、アメリカ人の場合は違います。それはペリー提督の時代から、今日でも変わりません。

During the Edo era, in Japan gold coinage was traded to silver at a rate of 1 to 3. The actual world rate was 1 to 16. When foreigners first came to Japan at the end of the Edo era, they were quick to notice this. Westerners cheated Japanese people. Even the first American ambassador, Townsend Harris, made a lot of money in this fashion. No foreigner told the Japanese government how badly they were being cheated. It was only when the various Fiefs, and later the Meiji government, sent Japanese students abroad that this scam was discovered.

　江戸時代に、日本では金貨は銀へ１対３で交換されていましたが、世界のレートは１対16でした。江戸時代の最後、幕末に日本へきた外国人は、このレートの違いにすぐ気付きました。その違いに気付いた外国人は日本人を騙し続けました。初代駐日アメリカ大使タウンゼント・ハリスはこのレートの違いを利用した詐

欺でとても儲けました。外国人は誰一人として、日本人が騙されている事を、日本政府に忠告することはありませんでした。その後、徐々に諸藩や明治政府が日本人研究者を海外へ派遣するようになってから、日本人はこの詐欺に気付きました。

Today, many foreigners who come to Japan have some kind of plan to pull something over on Japanese people. During the bubble years, many foreigners came to Japan with all kinds of stories. There is a phrase in English. "If people are dumb enough to buy it, I am smart enough to sell it." This means that it is OK to cheat a person, or sell substandard merchandise. Of course, there is no concept of this in Japanese society.

I personally knew of some Japanese women who were conned out their savings. Many foreigners got English teaching jobs with fake credentials. I had heard that anyone could get a fake university degree in Bangkok or Taipei. And they would then use that to get a teaching visa in Japan.

　現在、日本に来る外国人は数多く、何かと日本人を騙す計画を持っています。バブル時代に嘘の話を持ち込む外国人はたくさん居ました。英語のフレーズがあります。「もし愚かな人がこれを買うのであれば、賢い私はそれを売る」これは、人を騙しても、或いは、品質が悪い物を売っても大丈夫だということです。勿論、日本社会にこういう考えは有りません。

　私は個人的に、何人かの日本人女性が外国人から自分の貯金を騙しとられたという話を聞いた事が有ります。数多くの外国人は偽造の大学卒業証書で、英語教師の仕事を得ています。ある外国人から聞いた話では台北とかバンコクで簡単に偽造の大学卒業証書を作ることが出来るとのことでした。彼らはそれを使って日本で英語の先生のビザを得ています。

Chapter 1 Japan, 161 years in the shadow of the Black Ships

Just the other day, I was having some beer in an English pub in Tokyo. Talking to the young woman working behind the bar, she said she didn't like foreigners. "Why?" I asked. Her answer was that they always cheat. When she tells them that a certain drink costs ¥700, many foreigners answer with "Oh but it was ¥500 when I came last time". "NO! You must pay ¥700!"

先日、東京の英国パブでビールを飲みました。そのパブで働いている日本人女性と話をすると、彼女は外国人が嫌いだと言いました。「何故？」私が聞くと、彼女の答えは外国人はいつも人を騙すからということでした。例えば、「この飲み物は700円です」と言うと、外国人は「ええ！この前の時は500円でしたよ！」と言ってきます。彼女は強い声で、「違います。700円お支払いください！」というやりとりを、いちいちしなければならないということでした。

I had a similar experience. I used to work at a music live bar in Tokyo. One day, on my day off, the owner called me to come in, they were having trouble. That day there was popular Irish band in Tokyo playing. The customers were not paying the live charge of ¥1,000. They would have some story about having been in the bar a few minutes before, that they already paid. The Japanese person at the door could not speak English well, and he was intimidated by loud foreigners.

So I arrived and saw what was going on, my approach to a foreigner just arriving was "Hi! Can I get you a drink?" Well they were Irish so of course they answered yes. I would get them their drink, charge them for the drink, and say, "Oh, and the music charge is ¥1,000!"

They gave me angry looks, but they paid. I am a former US Marine, and I can look mean when I have to.

第1章　黒船の陰に有る161年間の日米関係

　私も同じ様な経験が有ります。昔、東京のあるライブハウスで働いていた時のことですが、ある休みの日、店長から「トラブルがあったので、店に来てくれないか？」という電話がありました。その日は東京で人気のアイルランド人バンドのライブでした。お客の外国人は1,000円のライブチャージを払っていません。しかし「私は前にチャージを払いました！」と強気で嘘を言い、受付に居た日本人はあまり英語が話せず、うるさく強気な外国人に押されて負けています。

　私はお店に着いてこれを見て、こう対応しました。まず着いたばかりの外国人に「何かお飲み物は？」と聞きます。アイルランド人でしたから、勿論、何か飲みますので、飲み物を渡す時に、「ライブチャージは1,000円です！」と言いました。

　私に対していやな顔をしましたが、彼らは払いました。私は元米海兵隊ですから、厳しい表情を作ることが出来ます。

　That night there were 100 customers in the bar, but only 30 paid the live charge. But they were not cheating only the bar, they were cheating the band, most of that money was for the band.

　I could hear the comments of many people, they thought they were very funny by avoiding payment of the live charge.

　その夜、お客様は100人位でしたが、結局たったの30人しかチャージを払っていません。彼らは店を騙すだけではなく、友達のバンドはチャージの8割を受けるのですから、自分の友達も平気で騙しているのです。

　そのお客様達の考えを聞いてみると、自分がチャージを払わずに逃れられるということは、自分らが頭が良いということであり、騙される日本人は滑稽だと言っていました。

　In America, people never believe what a person says, they check.

Chapter 1 Japan, 161 years in the shadow of the Black Ships

For example, if you apply for a job in America, many companies will ask for references. And they will call those people to ask what kind of person you are.

　アメリカでは、多くの人は人の話をそのまま信じません。まず本当のことであるのかを確認します。例えば、もしも貴方がアメリカの会社に就職を申し込む場合、推薦が必要です。その会社は必ずその推薦人に連絡して、貴方がどういう人なのかということを聞き、調査をします。

In business, a person should be careful in dealing with Americans. Too many Japanese people think Americans can be trusted. Not at all. That is why America is such a legalistic society. In any transaction, everything must be spelled out exactly in contract.

Violation of these conditions brings penalties. In Japan, people can do business with a handshake. If a person in Japan does live up to the conditions of the agreement, well he loses trust, and his reputation is damaged.

　ビジネスの場合、アメリカ人と商取引をする時は注意した方が良いです。アメリカ人をそのまま信用出来ると考えている日本人が多過ぎます。全くそんなことはありません。だから、アメリカは完全に法的な社会なのです。どんな活動でも、厳密に契約書を書く必要がありますので、その内容に注意しなければなりません。

　アメリカでは、契約書の条件を守らなかったり、違反をすると、必ず法律で裁かれ罰を受けます。日本の場合は商売の交渉は何も契約をせず、お互いの同意（約束）で決める事が多く、同意を守らない場合、その人が信用を失います。

In America, if there is trouble, the person who trusted someone would be at fault. I worry very much about the TPP negotiations for Japan. Japanese people just do not have such a legalistic mind. In Japan, relationships are much more important. Americans easily lie. If no one finds out, then there is no sense of wrong doing. The person who is cheated is at fault. For that reason, America is a country of laws that are strictly enforced. But is this truly a wonderful thing? No, it isn't.

For the American the exact legal agreement is much more important than personal friendship or connection. And that is why Americans are such lonely people.

アメリカでは、問題があった場合、人を信用する人が悪いとなります。この理由からもTPPは本当に心配です。日本人はアメリカ人のような法律的な考え方があまり有りません。日本の場合は、人間関係の方が大切だからです。アメリカ人は平気で嘘をつきます。嘘はバレなければ良く、罪の意識などありません。詐欺は騙される方が悪いという考えです。その為にアメリカは法律が厳しく訴訟社会です。これは素晴らしい考えですか。全く違います。

アメリカ人にとっては、人の縁とか友情より法的な同意の方がずっと大切です。こうしてみると、アメリカ人は寂しい人達ですね。

Illusion of Globalization
国際化の幻想

Some people still speak of the need for Japan to internationalize, to learn English, accept more foreigners in Japan, to learn foreign culture.

I disagree. We don't need foreigners at all. Japanese language ability should a requirement for a residence or work visa. And in work habits and methods, Japanese ways are superior. There

33

Chapter 1 Japan, 161 years in the shadow of the Black Ships

is nothing more Japan can learn from foreign countries. Rather, Japan should teach proper ways of management to other countries. And that includes America, it is becoming a non functional country.

　日本ではまだ、日本は国際化が必要、まず英語を覚えることが必要、他国の文化を勉強する必要が有るという話を聞きます。
　違います。外国人は全然必要有りません。それよりも、日本で働くことが出来るビザや永住権は、日本語が出来ることを必須にするべきです。仕事のやり方、習慣は、日本人の方が優れています。外国から、日本人が学べる事ももうたいして有りません。逆に、日本は適切な経営方法を外国に教えるべきです。それもアメリカを含めてです。残念ながら、アメリカはだんだん非機能的な国になっていますので。

Well, back in Commodore Perry's time, what did Americans think of Japan? Most Americans didn't know much about Japan, and that is still true today.

At the American centennial international exhibition held in Philadelphia in 1876, the Japanese exhibition was very popular with American people. A Japanese house and shop were erected. Americans greatly admired the crafts, such as lacquer ware. But among Americans the admiration of Japanese art, craftsmanship, and culture remained confined to American elites. And in America elite people are not respected.

To follow intellectual pursuits in American society is regarded as effeminate. Physically weak. To be effeminate for Americans is to be like a homosexual. And most Americans regard a homosexual as someone who should be bullied or killed.

So in a cultural sense, it is hard for the average American to be attracted by Japanese culture.

34

第 1 章　黒船の陰に有る 161 年間の日米関係

　さて、ペリー提督の時代に、ほとんどのアメリカ人が日本の事について何も知らなかったのですが、その状態は現在でも同じです。

　1876 年、アメリカのフィラデルフィア万国博覧会で、日本家屋と日本の店舗が造られた日本の展示はとても人気がありました。アメリカ人は日本の手工芸品、特に漆物を称賛しました。その日本の芸術に感嘆している人は、アメリカ人の中でも上流階級の人士のみでした。しかし、アメリカでは、そのようなエリートの人達は尊敬されていません。

　現在でも、アメリカで知的な事を勉強する事は、肉体的に弱く男らしくないと考えられています。アメリカでは、男らしくないということは、同性愛者であると考えられます。そして、だいたいのアメリカ人は同性愛者は虐められるべきで、もっと言うと殺されるべき人であると考えています。

　ですから、一般的なアメリカ人の感覚では、日本文化を魅力的であると捉える事は難しいでしょう。

 However there is one aspect of Japanese culture that is very popular among Americans, that is martial arts. Americans who study marital arts say that they truly understand Bushido, but I have doubts.   Modern day Americans think too much of martial arts as some kind of super power, where a person can perform miraculous feats and destroy an opponent.

　しかし、日本文化でも、アメリカでとても人気が高い事があります。それは武術です。武術を学んでいるアメリカ人は武士道を理解していると言いますが、私はそれを疑ってしまいます。現在のアメリカ人は、武術をとても強大な力と捉えていて、その奇跡的な力を使って相手を倒すことが出来ると考えているからです。

Chapter 1 Japan, 161 years in the shadow of the Black Ships

Geisha and sex
芸者とセックス

One other aspect that Americans dream about Japan is Geisha. Of course they have no actual concept of what a Geisha is, but they think of the sex. The average American believes that a Geisha has ways of touching a man that are like magic, and can bring a man to instant sexual ecstasy.

　I think one of the reasons that American men dream of Geisha is because American women are so difficult. They are constantly trying to show that they are superior to men, and demand constant attention and praise from men. Also, American women always belittle men.

　もう一つのアメリカ人が日本に夢想している事は、芸者です。勿論、芸者がどういう存在かは全然分かっておらず、ただセックスの事しか考えていないのです。普通のアメリカ人は、日本の芸者は、男性に対して魔法のような触れる技術を持っていて、男性は突然、性的頂点に導かれると考えています。

　アメリカ人がそんな風に日本の芸者に幻想を抱いている理由は、アメリカ人女性が非常に厳しいからです。いつも自分が男より優れていると示そうとしていて、常に男から注目されたいし、称賛するように男性に要求します。アメリカ女性はいつも男性を貶します。

Americans have very strange ideas concerning sex, they are afraid of it. Well, a lot of this is because American Christianity often tends toward very harsh strains of thought. In American Christianity, sex is thought of as simply evil. Actually, America is a very sexually repressed country. Europeans don't seem to have the same complexes towards sex that Americans do, and Europe is basically Christian.

　アメリカ人はセックスについて変な考え方をたくさん持っていて、セックスを恐れています。一つの理由は、アメリカのキリスト教は厳しい宗派が多いということです。アメリカのキリスト教ではセックスは単純に悪です。実はアメリカは性的に抑圧されている国なのです。ヨーロッパ人はアメリカ人の様なセックスコンプレックスは無いでしょう。

But for an American man who visits Japan, and meets Japanese women, Japan is a candy store. It is very easy to have sex with Japanese women if they fell in love with you, and Japanese women do not have all the demands American women make. Well, what do I mean, Japan is a "candy store"? Some American men just go crazy here. I remember some years back, I had an audition for a TV commercial in Akasaka, Tokyo. At the audition, I met an American Air Force person from Yokota air base.

We walked back to the station together. Near Akasaka Mitsuke

American image of Geisha
アメリカ人の芸者のイメージです
出典：映画「The Barbarian and the Geisha」(1958)

Chapter 1 Japan, 161 years in the shadow of the Black Ships

station, there was a very beautiful women, wearing a very form clinging dress. She had a tattoo on her arm. Obviously, she was a hostess in some nearby club. This ignorant American walks up to her, grabs her arm and says "Hi I want to talk to you!" My reaction was immediate. "Knock it off you fool!"

　しかし、日本に来て日本人女性と出会えるアメリカ人男性にとって、日本は〝キャンディーストア〟です。日本人女性は、その人を好きになれば、条件無しで気軽にセックスして、アメリカ人女性の様にたくさんの要求はしないからです。〝キャンディーストア〟とは、子供が入り浸りで夢中になる店のことです。これと同じ様に、日本では魅力的な日本人女性によって何人ものアメリカ人男性の頭がおかしくなってしまうからです。数年前に東京の赤坂でテレビ CM のオーディションが有り、そのオーディションで、横田基地の米空軍の人に会いました。

　私たちは一緒に駅まで歩きましたが、赤坂見附駅の近くの路上に、ボディコンのドレスを着た美しい日本人が居ました。腕に入れ墨が有り、どこか近くのクラブで働いている事は明らかでした。この無知なアメリカ人はその彼女のところへ行き、腕をつかんで、「こんにちは！私は貴方と話したいです！」と言いだしたので、私は咄嗟に「バカ！やめろ！」と声をあげました。

American women in a demonstration
デモを行なっているアメリカ人女性です

38

第 1 章　黒船の陰に有る 161 年間の日米関係

But this idiot American apparently felt that all Japanese women were available for him to have sex on demand. In America, such an action would be a crime, sexual assault.

Also, in general, many American women are overweight. Japanese women are generally slim, attractive, and dress well. Some Asian Americans call this sexual obsession with Asian women as "Yellow Fever".

　この愚かなアメリカ人は、全ての日本人女性はいつでも簡単に彼とセックスをしてくれると考えていました。アメリカではそのような行動は、性的暴行、犯罪です。

　それから、一般的にアメリカ女性は太っています。ほとんどの日本女性は痩せていて、魅力的ですし、服のセンスも良いです。アジア系アメリカ人は、この様なアジア女性とのセックスが病みつきになる事を〝黄熱病〟と呼びます。

However, there is one great mistake Americans make about Japanese women. It may be easy to date and have sex with a Japanese woman. Almost always, the American man will fall head over heels in love with the girl, and propose marriage. However for Japanese people, marriage is a very important thing. And it involves the family.

In general, American family ties are just not that strong compared to Japan. And this baffles many Americans. I have often heard American men say how prejudiced Japanese are, because some man could not get permission to marry from a girl's family.

Well, it is also hard for Japanese to get married sometimes. A man's income can be a decisive factor. But as usual, Americans do not observe the Japanese society around them, but make quick

39

Chapter 1 Japan, 161 years in the shadow of the Black Ships

judgements. And in their quick judgement, America is always superior.

　でも、アメリカ人男性が日本人女性を大きく勘違いしてしまう事があります。外国人が、日本人女性とデートしたりセックスをするのは簡単かもしれません。そうすると、アメリカ人男性の方はすっかり惚れ込んですぐに結婚のプロポーズをします。しかし、日本人の場合、結婚はとても大切な事です。家族も深く関わってきます。

　一般的にアメリカの家族の絆は日本のようには深くありません。アメリカ人はこの真実を理解出来ず当惑します。私が話を聞いた多くのアメリカ人男性は、日本人は差別的だと言います。何故なら、日本人女性の家族から結婚を許可してもらえなかったからです。

　もちろん、日本人同士でも結婚が難しいことはあるでしょう。男性の収入は大切です。しかし、いつもの様に、アメリカ人は日本の社会を見ないで、性急な判断をします。そして、その性急な判断では、常にアメリカの方が優れていると判断します。

 So I think that today, we can say that there are really only two areas that Americans have interest in Japan, they see Japan as a violent nation, full of martial artist Samurai, and full of sexual women.

　このように、現在、アメリカ人は基本的に日本に対して、二つの事だけに興味が有ります。アメリカ人の考えでは、日本は武術家や侍、それと数多くの気軽にセックスしてくれる女性のいる乱暴な国であるということです。

第 1 章　黒船の陰に有る 161 年間の日米関係

Uneducated Americans
教養のないアメリカ人

In 161 years of relations with Japan, Americans have learned virtually nothing about Japan.

The opposite is certainly not true. When I first came to Japan 40 years ago, I was amazed at how much Japanese people knew about America. Often, I would meet Japanese people who knew more American history than Americans do. And sometimes, Japanese people who spoke better English than Americans. This will surprise many Japanese people, but it is true, more and more Americans cannot speak English. Well, what then do they speak? Gibberish.

Just the other night I was out having drinks with some people. I mentioned that many prominent Americans cannot communicate in English. President Bush was famous for this. Sarah Pailin, a candidate for Vice President of the United States in 2008, was absolutely incomprehensible. Well, how could she be so popular? That is because many Americans are ignorant like her. Newspapers would devote articles trying to interpret what she was saying.

　日米関係の 161 年間で、アメリカ人は日本の事をほとんど何も学んでいません。

　逆は違います。私は 40 年前に初めて日本へ来た時に、日本人がアメリカの文化、歴史などにとても深い知識を持っていることに驚きました。アメリカ人よりアメリカの歴史に詳しい日本人に何人も会いました。時々、普通のアメリカ人より英語が上手い日本人にも会いました。日本人はこの話に驚くかも知れませんが、だんだん、まともな英語を話せないアメリカ人が増えています。

Chapter 1 Japan, 161 years in the shadow of the Black Ships

　それでは、普通のアメリカ人はどういう言葉を喋っているのか？
　はっきり言ってチンプンカンプンです。
　先日、友達とお酒を飲んだ時に、多くのアメリカの著名人は英語でコミュニケーションが出来ない、という話をしました。ブッシュ大統領は英語が下手で有名でした。それから、2008年大統領選挙の共和党副大統領候補者サラ・ペイリンさんの英語は全く理解不能です。それでは、どうして彼女はそんなに人気があるのでしょうか？　その理由は、ほとんどのアメリカ人は彼女と同じ様な無知な人ばかりだからです。当時の新聞記事の内容は、全て彼女の言いたいことを推測し解釈したものでした。

And so many Japanese try hard to study English and other languages. In America, almost nobody speaks a language other than English, they have no interest. And most Americans don't speak English well.

However, I must say that in the 40 years I have lived in Japan, I have seen educational standards start to fall. I think that Japanese have too much exposure to Americans.

　一方、多くの日本人は一所懸命に英語や他の言葉を勉強します。アメリカでは、英語以外の言葉を出来る人はほとんどいません。アメリカ人は英語以外の言葉に興味が有りません。それでも、ほとんどのアメリカ人は英語を上手に話すことは出来ませんが。

　しかし、私が日本に住んでいる40年間で、日本の教育基準は低下していると言えるでしょう。この原因は日本がアメリカとの縁が深くなり過ぎているからでしょう。

Fear of Japan
日本に対する恐れ

 Also Americans fear Japan. Americans are a violent people, so inevitably they think Japanese, with a Bushido culture, must be violent too. So Japan must be destroyed or controlled. Personally, I call this the "Mirror Effect". Americans can only try to think of other cultures as being what Americans themselves are. Americans are violent, so Japanese must be violent too.

 それと、アメリカ人は日本を恐れています。アメリカ人は暴力的な国民ですから、彼らは武士道文化が有る日本人も必然的に暴力的な民族であると思っているのです。私はこの考え方を〝ミラー効果〟と呼びます。アメリカ人は他国の文化を考える時に、自分と似ているだろうとしか考えません。アメリカ人は暴力的、だから、日本人もそうだろう、と解釈します。

 This is the reason that America annexed Hawaii. It was fear of Japan. In 1893, there were 2,000 Americans living in Hawaii. Mostly, they were businessmen, who owned fruit plantations on the island. There were some 20,000 Japanese who worked on these plantations. There were other nationalities who worked in the Hawaiian islands, such as Filipinos and Chinese, but the American business class feared the Japanese people.

 They feared Japan because they assumed Japanese people would act like Americans, and attempt to dominate Hawaii by force. They imagined that many of the Japanese laborers were actually secret agents of the Imperial Japanese Army, waiting for their chance to attack.

Chapter 1 Japan, 161 years in the shadow of the Black Ships

　この理由で、アメリカはハワイを併合しました。日本への恐れです。1893年にハワイに2千人のアメリカ人が住んでいました。ほとんどの場合が、ハワイの果実農園を所有しているビジネスマンでした。このハワイの農園で2万人の日本人労働者が働いていました。ハワイでは他の民族も、例えば、フィリピン人と中国人も働いていました。しかし、アメリカ人のビジネスマンは日本人を恐れました。
　その日本人を恐れた理由は、日本人はアメリカ人の様に強制的にハワイを支配しようとすると仮定していたからです。アメリカ人が想像していたのは、この日本人労働者は、実は日本帝国陸軍の軍人であり、アメリカ人に対して攻撃が出来るチャンスを待っていると考えていました。

So the American planters struck first. They convinced the captains of several American Naval vessels present in Hawaii to send their Marines to depose the Hawaiian Queen. The US government in Washington had no knowledge of this action.

The reason Americans feared Japan, and not China, was that Meiji Japan was quickly becoming a modern state. Americans fear equality. They must always be the dominant entity in any group.

　それで先にアメリカ人農園主が動きました。ハワイに停泊しているアメリカ海軍の軍艦の船長達を説得して、その海兵隊を借りて、ハワイの女王様を強制的に解任しました。ワシントンのアメリカ政府はこの行動を知りませんでした。
　アメリカが日本を恐れ中国を恐れなかった理由は、明治の日本は急速に近代的な産業国になっていたということです。アメリカ人は平等の立場を恐れます。どんなグループでも、アメリカ人は一番強い立場でいなければならないのです。

Japan did send a warship to investigate the situation, the Naniwa under the command of Togo Heihachiro. The Japanese officers conferred with officers of American ships in the harbor, and war was averted. But China at that time could not offer any challenge to America, this is why Americans feared Japan. As time went on in the Japanese relationship, this combination of American fear and desire to dominate defined the relationship.

   At the time of the American annexation of Hawaii, most Americans inside the United States proper did not really fear Japan. However with the Japanese victory over Russia in the Russo-Japanese war, this changed.

   明治政府が、ハワイの状況を調べる為に、帝国海軍の東郷平八郎指揮の下、軍艦「浪速」をハワイへ派遣しました。そして、ハワイ港停泊中のアメリカ海軍の士官たちと浪速の士官達が会談、協議して、戦争を回避しました。しかし、当時、中国はアメリカに抵抗することが出来ませんでした。それもあり、アメリカ人は日本を恐れました。時間がたつにつれ、この恐れと日本を支配し

US troops in Honolulu Hawaii at overthrow of monarchy 1893
1893年、ハワイモナーキー（王国）を崩壊させているアメリカ軍人です
出典：Hawaii State Archives

Chapter 1 Japan, 161 years in the shadow of the Black Ships

たいという気持ちが日米関係の形を決めました。
　ハワイ併合の時に、アメリカ本土に住んでいるアメリカ人は特に日本への恐れはありませんでしたが、日露戦争における日本の勝利でその気持ちが変わったのです。

Now Japan, a non white, non Christian nation, had defeated a white Christian nation in war. At the same time, Japanese people began to settle in California. Very quickly, there were conflicts. Japanese people worked hard. They worked harder than Americans, in farming and as small shopkeepers in direct competition with Americans. And Americans reacted badly. There were increasing number of laws restricting the activity including the businesses of Japanese people.

Today, with TPP, we can see the same type of action. American car companies are terrified of the Japanese Kei car. So they try to create laws to destroy it. Despite TPP supposedly being a free trade agreement, the Kei car is still restricted in America. Next, America will try to restrict it's use in Japan.

After that, with TPP Americans will create laws to force Japanese people to use American cars in Japan. The idea to work harder and create a car suitable for the Japanese market just does not occur to Americans. They will try to force Japan to use American cars.

　さて、白人でもキリスト教国でもない日本が、戦争で白人、キリスト教国のロシアを破りました。そしてその頃、日本人はカリフォルニアに定住し始めていました。すぐに衝突が起こりました。日本人はよく働きました。日本人は農業でも商業でもアメリカ人より一生懸命働いたので、直接ビジネスの競争相手となったのです。アメリカ人の反応はひどいものでした。徐々に日本人の商売をはじめ、様々な活動を禁止する法律を作ったのです。

現在行なわれているTPPの交渉でも、同じような発想が見えます。アメリカの車メーカーは日本の軽自動車が邪魔な存在で恐れています。おそらく軽自動車を潰すルールを作るでしょう。TPPは自由貿易条約と言われていますが、軽自動車はアメリカでは制限されています。次に、アメリカは日本で軽自動車を制限しようとするでしょう。

その後、TPPの内容に合わせる形で、アメリカの車メーカーは日本人が強制的にアメリカの車を買う様にルールを作るでしょう。もっと頑張って日本市場に合う車を造るという発想は、アメリカ人には考え付きません。強制的な力を利用して、日本人にアメリカの車を買わせるでしょう。

In recent times, the only non white people to beat white people in war are Japanese. This is why there is still strong anti Japanese feeling in the United States. Since Americans themselves are very aggressive, they imagine that their opponent must also be so.

近代で白人に抵抗し、勝利した有色人種は日本人だけです。今もアメリカ人の中には日本人に払拭できない根本的な恐れがあります。しかし、アメリカ人自身が戦闘的な為に、相手もそうであるという幻想が恐怖を増幅させています。

Immigrants and society
移民と社会

Here, I will write a little about immigration in Japan and America. If you see my name, it is obvious that my ancestry is German. But my mother was Swedish. She was born in America, but her parents, my grandparents, came from Sweden to America.

Chapter 1 Japan, 161 years in the shadow of the Black Ships

When I told my grandfather that I would emigrate to Japan, he got very angry. When he came to America, he had many tough experiences. People treated him like a fool because he could not speak English, because he was not born in the United States. When I told him I could go to Japan and teach English, making good money, he could not believe me.

これから、日本とアメリカの移民について比較したいと思います。私の名字を読むと、私がドイツ系であることは明らかです。しかし、私の母方はスウェーデン系でした。彼女はアメリカに生まれましたが、彼女の親、つまり私の祖父母は、スウェーデンからアメリカへ海を渡りました。

スウェーデンの祖父に、私は日本に移民すると言いますと、彼はとても怒りました。彼はアメリカへ移民した時に、多くの厳しい経験をしていたのです。アメリカ生まれでなかったために英語が出来ないということで、アメリカ人から愚か者扱いされていたのです。私は日本へ行けば、英語を教えて、良いお金を貰う事が出来ると話しましたが、彼は私の話を信じることが出来ませんでした。

Myself, I have had the experience of emigrating into America. It is very hard. Having lived in Japan for 20 years, I was treated as a non American immigrant by Americans. Americans do not care what experience you have had in another country. To Americans, if you were not employed by an American company, you were unemployed. I speak fluent Japanese. But for work in Japan, I was told by Americans that speaking Japanese only made me a talking dog.

私はアメリカへ移民した事が有ります。その手続きはとても困難でした。私はアメリカ人ですが日本に２０年住んでいたので、

アメリカ人から外国生まれの移民の人と同じ扱いをされました。アメリカ人は別の国でどのような経験があったとしても評価しません。アメリカ人にとっては、アメリカの会社で働いた事がなければ、貴方は失業者です。私は日本語を上手く話すことが出来ます。しかし、日本で働く為に、日本語を話せるようにする事で、私はアメリカ人から只の喋る犬と言われました。

TPP - American way of doing business
TPP- アメリカ式ビジネスのやり方

I had such an experience in New York City 20 years ago. I was at a headhunters office. They knew of an American company who wished to base a sales representative for 2 years in Sapporo Japan.

Well I told the staff of my experience working in Japan, how I had sold Japanese electronics in Southeast Asia. How I had lived in Japan for 20 years, spoke fluent Japanese, understood Japanese business culture.

The headhunter then asked me about my MBA. Well I had studied political science at International Christian University in Tokyo. I was then asked what American companies I had worked for. When I said that I had worked for Japanese companies, I was told that such experience was worthless.

　私が20年前にニューヨークで経験したことをお話ししましょう。私はヘッドハンターの事務所へ行きました。その事務所の情報で、2年間日本の札幌へ営業マンを派遣したいと考えているアメリカの会社があるということを知ったからです。
　そこのスタッフに私の経歴を説明しました。私は東南アジアで日本の電化製品を販売した事が有り、日本に20年間住んでいたので、日本語を上手く話すことが出来ますし、日本のビジネス文

Chapter 1 Japan, 161 years in the shadow of the Black Ships

化を理解しているということを説明しました。
　そのヘッドハンター事務所のスタッフは、私のMBAについて尋ねたので、私は、東京の国際基督教大学で政治学を勉強した事が有る、という回答をしました。次の質問は、「どこかアメリカの会社で働いた事が有りますか？」でした。私が、日本の会社で働いていましたと回答すると、そのスタッフが、「そういう経験は価値が有りません」と言いました。

　Well I did not get the job. But what this company will do is send some person who has an MBA, understands American business theory. But this person will have no idea of how to function in Japan.
　In the two years this person was supposed to spend in Japan, they would just begin to get an idea of how to deal with Japanese people. And then be replaced by another person, who knows nothing and has to learn from scratch. And of course, the products the company is trying are unlikely to be attractive to Japanese consumers.

　結局、私はその仕事をすることが出来ませんでした。しかし、その会社はMBAを持っていて、アメリカビジネス理論を知っている人であれば、その人を日本へ派遣します。でも、その人は日本でどういう風にビジネスを展開したら良いか分かりません。
　その人が日本で働く２年間で、日本人とのビジネスのやり方が少しずつ分かると思います。その期間が終わると、その人はアメリカへ帰り、また新しく何も知らない人が来ます。そして勿論、そのやり方では、アメリカの会社が日本に売りたい商品は、日本の消費者にとって魅力はないでしょう。

　In such a case, Americans will always say that the fault is on the

Japanese side. They think there must be some invisible barrier that keeps Japanese people from buying their product. This is the basis of the TPP trade agreement. The American side will use the power of their government to force Japanese to buy their products.

If you try to tell them that Japanese will have no use for their product, or that their product does not fit the Japanese market, they will not listen. And then they will use force. So TPP is really not at all about free trade. It is about American corporations using the power of the US government to force their products upon Japan and the world, even if we don't want them.

そのような場合、アメリカ人はいつも日本が悪いと言います。何やら見えない障壁があって、そのせいで日本人はアメリカの製品を買わないのだと言います。TPP の基本はこれです。アメリカ側は自分達の政府の力を利用して、強制的に日本人にアメリカの商品を買わせるという事です。

アメリカ人に、君達が作っている商品が日本に合わないし日本人は使いたいと思わない、という事を言っても聞きません。それで強制的な力を利用します。ですから、TPP とは自由貿易には関係なく、世界の国々がアメリカの商品を買いたくなくても、アメリカ企業がアメリカ政府の力を利用して強制的に買わせるというシステムです。

It is much easier to get a job in Japan than America. What is important in a Japanese company is ability to get along well with other people, and willingness to work hard and learn. And Japanese people are much kinder to foreigners than Americans. People in Japan try to help you fit into the local community. In America, you are at first welcomed, then ignored. And there is very little sense of community in America, it is a lonely country.

Chapter 1 Japan, 161 years in the shadow of the Black Ships

　日本では、アメリカより仕事を見つけやすいです。日本の会社で大切な事は、他の社員と仲良く一生懸命働く事と、勉強する気持ちです。それから、日本人はアメリカ人より外国人に優しいです。日本では、外国人がその地域社会に入る為の手伝いをしてくれます。アメリカでは最初「ようこそ」と言って歓迎されますが、その後はほとんど無視されます。アメリカには共同社会という意識がほとんどありません。とても寂しい国です。

The Emperor and the Imperial Household
天皇と皇室

　But there is one more thing I want to write here. Why did Japan succeed in creating a country that could resist foreign demands, when other countries could not? I think the key to Japanese success is the Imperial Household. It provided a point of unity that all Japanese could rally around.

　ここでもう一つ大切な事を書こうと思います。江戸幕府の開国後、他国には出来なかった、外国の要求に抵抗出来る、新しい政府を作ることに、何故、日本は成功したのでしょうか？　私の考えでは、日本が成功した一番重要な理由は、皇室です。皇室は、日本全国の国民を１つにまとめることが出来る存在でした。

　China attempted to resist foreign domination, but regionalistic forces were too strong. The Qing emperor simply did not provide a unifying force. China remained divided, and foreigners could easily dominate China.

　In Korea, the rulers simply tried to maintain their isolation. They tried to protect their static and unchanging society that was basically a slave society. This policy failed completely. If Japan had not annexed and modernized Korea, it would have become a Russian colony. If that had happened, South Korea would have never become a sovereign nation today

　中国は外国の要求や支配に抵抗しようとしましたが、地方毎の力が強過ぎたので、清朝は統一された力にはなりませんでした。中国はそのまま国内が分裂して、外国人が簡単に支配することが出来ました。
　朝鮮では、支配者達は閉鎖的な政策を守り、自分達の為に、保守的な進化しない奴隷制に支えられた腐敗した社会をそのまま続けようとしました。これは、完全に失敗でした。もし、日本が朝鮮を併合し近代化しなかったら、朝鮮はロシアの植民地になっていたでしょう。そうなっていたら、以後二度と再び朝鮮人の自治は生じなかったでしょう。

Americans just cannot understand what the Japanese Emperor is. They keep thinking of an absolute ruler, in the European sense. No! The Japanese Emperor is a spiritual being, who represents all Japanese people. The Emperor does not issue orders or commands. Simply by existing, the Japanese Emperor provides guidance to the people of Japan.

This may be a very abstract concept for Western people to consider, but may I remind them that Japan is a different civilization than the West. Westerners simply cannot comprehend the true nature of the Japanese Emperor. Westerners should try to understand things beyond their basic beliefs. Things they cannot understand they fear.

　アメリカ人は、天皇陛下はどんな存在であるかという事を理解出来ません。ヨーロッパの独裁者の様な存在であると永遠に考え

ています。しかしそれは違います。日本の天皇陛下は聖的ですし、すべての日本国民を代表する精神的な存在です。命令などはしません。存在だけで、日本国民に将来の道を示しています。

　西洋人にとって、これは抽象的な考え方かも知れません。しかし、日本は西洋の国とは違う文明の国です。西洋人は天皇を全く理解していませんし、おそらく理解できない存在でもあります。西洋人は自分の理解を越えるものがあることを受け入れるべきです。しかし、理解できないことが恐れになります。

Japan-Korea dispute
日韓問題

I would now like to address the Korean situation. As I have written, when Westerners poured into Northeast Asia, Japan coped with the situation by creating a new society, Meiji Japan.

On the other hand, the reaction of the Korean rulers was to seek to strengthen their isolation. The thing was, at the time, intelligent people could see that the prevailing social order could not last in the face of foreign intrusion. There were people in Korea who understood this, and wanted to emulate Japan's success. However, the pro Japanese activists were executed and suppressed by the Korean government.

　そこで、現在の日韓問題について書こうと思います。私が書いてきた様に、西洋人が東アジアに押し寄せた時に、日本はこの大変困難な状況に上手く対処し、新しい社会、明治日本を作りました。

　一方、朝鮮の支配者達の反応は、ますます孤立する閉鎖的な政策を続ける事でした。当時の朝鮮の知識人は、外国人の強制的な侵入に対して抵抗する術がなく、今まで通りの政策が不可能であると感じていました。彼らは、日本の明治維新の成功を真似した

いと考えました。しかし、親日派の彼らは朝鮮政府に抑制されて、粛清されました。

After that, Japan annexed and modernized Korea. The Korean script, Hangul, was revived by Japanese scholars, and taught to the general populace. In fact, Japan established universal and modern education in Korea.

At the time of Commodore Perry's arrival, some 70% of Japanese men and women could read and write. In Europe or America, the average was 40%. In Korea the literacy rate was very low. Japan changed that. Japan built railroads, created a postal system. All these things the Korean government refused to do, or could not do.

その後、日本が朝鮮を併合し朝鮮の近代化を実行しました。朝鮮の文字ハングルは、日本の学者が朝鮮社会に復活させて、一般の朝鮮人に教えました。実は、日本が朝鮮における一般的な近代教育制度を確立しました。

ペリー提督が来日した頃に、ヨーロッパやアメリカでの識字率は、平均で人口の約4割でしたが、日本人は人口の約7割もありました。朝鮮の識字率はとても低いものでした。日本がそれを変えました。そして日本は鉄道、郵便局等を造りました。このような国民の為の整備を実行することを、併合前の朝鮮政府は拒否し、また能力も有りませんでした。

Chapter 1 Japan, 161 years in the shadow of the Black Ships

Korea was not a colony of Japan
朝鮮は日本の植民地ではなかった

There is another very important fact here. Korea was not in any way a colony of Japan. Today, to gain sympathy from foreigners, Koreans use the phrase "Japan's brutal colonization" to describe the era.

A colonial relationship is a parasitical relationship. The powerful nation sucks the resources from the weak nation, like a Vampire in popular literature. The powerful nation creates little or no infrastructure in the subject nation, and does not concern itself with education of the populace.

As for Korea, when Japan annexed the country to the Japanese Empire, Koreans became equal in law. Of course there some difficulties, but no Western power, including America, has ever built such a constructive relationship with a subject nation.

　ここにもう一つの大切な真実が有ります。現在、外国人から同情を買う為に、〝日本の残忍な植民地時代〟という言葉を使っていますが、朝鮮は全く日本の植民地ではなかったということです。

　植民地の関係は寄生的な関係です。強国は、弱い国から資源をまるで吸血鬼の様に吸い取ります。強国は従属する国ではほとんどインフラを整備しないし、その国の国民の教育については気にしません。

　一方、朝鮮の場合では、日本は朝鮮を帝国に併合して、朝鮮人に対しても平等な法律で、彼らは日本帝国国民になりました。勿論、問題は有りましたが、西洋のどの国でも、アメリカを含めて、隷属国とこの様な建設的な関係を作ることはなかったのです。

Modern South Korea owes it's existence to Japanese help and goodwill. And the way South Koreans pay that back is to scream around the world how terrible Japan was, what victims they are.

As I write this, Korean groups are erecting monuments to what they call "Comfort Women" across the United States who, while they did exist, did not have the terrible lives that Korean activists claim. They are dragging Americans into their complexes about Japan, claiming that it is an international woman's right issue.

　現在の発展した韓国の存在は、日本の好意と援助が有ったから出来たことです。それなのに、現在の韓国人はその好意の返し方として、世界中に「日本がひどい！」「私たちは犠牲者だ！」と叫びます。
　私がこの文章を書いている時点で、在米韓国人団体はアメリカで現実には存在しなかった〝従軍慰安婦記念碑〟を建てています。韓国人団体は、この問題は国際的な女性の権利の問題であると主張し、自分たちが持っている日本に対する劣等コンプレックスに、アメリカを巻き込もうとしています。

Well, if Koreans are concerned about women's rights, perhaps then they should help the American FBI. One fourth of the women forcibly trafficked into prostitution in America are Korean. It is Korean groups that are doing this.

In particular, I am angry at Korean groups in America teaming up with Jewish groups in the United States to attack Japan. The Koreans are claiming the same status of victimhood as Jewish people. This is an outrageous lie, and an insult to the Jewish people. Most people in the United States don't know WWII history that well.

　もし、韓国人団体がそんなに国際的な女性の権利の問題を心配

Chapter 1 Japan, 161 years in the shadow of the Black Ships

しているのであれば、アメリカのFBIと協力するべきです。アメリカで強制的に売春、人身売買をされている女性の4分の1は、韓国人です。こういう行為を行なっているのは韓国人グループです。

特に、私が怒りを感じている事は、在米韓国人団体が日本を攻撃する為にユダヤ人と組んで、同じ様な戦争犠牲者であると言っていることに対してです。これは全くひどい嘘で、ユダヤ人に失礼です。ほとんどのアメリカ人は第二次世界大戦の歴史をそれほどよく分かっていません。

But Koreans prospered under Japanese rule, and willingly and ably fought for the Japanese Empire. Their present day actions in America are a gross deception. And discussing women's rights, as I have written here, it was Japan who began schooling for women. Before then, Korean women were literally slaves and did not have any human rights.

Comfort Women did exist, but they were basically voluntary paid prostitutes. Also, there were many unknowingly sold by their parents, or were deceived by a broker selling women, and were thus brought into the industry against their will. So the evil party here is that broker, or the girls parents, not the Japanese Army, or the Japanese government.

朝鮮人は日本統治のおかげで豊かな生活が有り、当時、日本帝国の為に、日本国民として一生懸命に戦いました。現在の在米活動は、完全に嘘です。女性の権利について言えば、朝鮮では日韓併合後、初めて日本が女性の為の学校を作ったのです。それまでは、女性は奴隷同然で何の権利も与えられていませんでした。

慰安婦は居ましたが、それは基本的に自分で志願して、高い給料を貰える売春でした。中には、知らないうちに親に売られていたり、女衒の甘言に騙された人もいて、それは本人の意思に反し

ていたでしょう。それはその人の親や悪い業者の責任であり、日本軍や政府の責任ではありません。

I have had personal experience with Koreans and their self centered view of history. Some 35 years ago, I used to live in Seoul. One day, some of my Korean friends asked me about WWII, and which country had the most difficult time in that war.

Well, I am a historian of that war, and my reply was Poland. My Korean friends were astonished, they replied that Korea and the most difficult time under Japanese rule.

Well, I answered, Poland was invaded by both Germany and the Soviet Union. Occupied by Germany for 5 years in which there was guerrilla warfare. The Jews of the ghetto in Warsaw revolted in 1943, the Polish Home Army revolted in Warsaw in 1944. The German Army fought desperately as the Soviet Army pushed through Poland towards Berlin. The Soviet Union forcibly changed Poland's borders after the war. All in all, 25% of the Polish population died in the war.

　私は、35年程前ソウルに住んでいた時に、韓国人が自分のことだけしか考えていないという、歴史の見方や考え方を持っているということを、目の当たりにした経験が有ります。ある日、何人かの韓国人の友人が、私に、「第二次世界大戦で、どこの国が最も厳しい戦争被害を受けたと思いますか？」という質問をしました。
　まあ、私は第二次世界大戦の歴史研究家ですから、その質問に対する回答はポーランドです。私の韓国人の友人達はとても驚いて、そうではない、韓国が、日本の支配のせいで最も辛く大変な国だったのだ、と言っていました。
　私はしっかりと説明しました。ポーランドはソ連とドイツの両国から侵略されていたこと、ドイツが占領した5年間は国内はゲリラ戦の戦場だったこと、1943年ユダヤ人ワルシャワ・ゲットー

Chapter 1 Japan, 161 years in the shadow of the Black Ships

蜂起、1944年ワルシャワ蜂起が国を崩壊させたこと。それから、ソ連軍がポーランドを通って、ベルリンに向かって進軍する際、追い込まれたドイツ軍が必死に抗戦した戦場であったことも。戦後、ソ連が強制的にポーランドの国境を変更しましたし、最終的に、ポーランドの人口の25％がその戦争で命を奪われたのです。

And I said that Korea suffered no air attacks in the war, comparatively speaking, it's experience was benign. My Korean friends began to scream and threaten to hit me. All they could think of was their own mythical idea of history. Other ideas were not to be discussed, just destroyed. They were then no longer my friends.

そして、朝鮮では空襲は無かったですし、大東亜戦争の経験はそこまで大変であるとは言えないでしょう、と。私の韓国人の友人は大声で怒鳴り、私に拳で殴りかかるような脅しをかけてきました。彼らは自分達の歴史認識、神話しか認められないので、その他の認識は議論することではなく、全て否定することしか出来ません。それで、私は彼らと縁を切りました。

Recently, the Korean government and media have created a massive propaganda campaign against Japan. There are mass rallies to protest against Japan. School students of all ages from kindergarten to university must attend these rallies in order to get good grades in school. Attendance is required in order to join a good company.

One of the obsessions is about the Tokdo/Takeshima dispute. It has been forcefully taken by the Korean military. But Koreans look ridiculous obsessing over what are really rocks as their sacred territory.

最近では、韓国の政府とマスコミは大規模な反日宣伝運動を作りあげ、日本に抗議する為の大集会もあります。おかしなことに、学校で良い成績を貰う為には、幼稚園から大学までの学生たちはこの集会に参加する必要がありますし、良い会社に就職する為にも、その集会に参加する必要があります。

　もう一つの妄想は独島・竹島(トクト)問題です。韓国軍が一方的に侵略して奪いました。しかし本当に、韓国人が只の岩を〝神聖な領土〟としていることは妄想で愚かなことであると思います。

 Korea has to grow up and understand other nations, and cease it's incessant psychological obsession with trying to prove they are better than Japan. Otherwise, they will become the laughingstock of the world.

　韓国はこれから他国を理解した方が良いでしょう。そして、日本に対する劣等感を裏返したような妄想を吐き出すことをやめて、世界に認められる大人の国になった方が良いです。そうしないと、本当に世界の笑いの種になりますよ。

第 2 章　戦争への道、中国に対する夢

Chapter 2　The road to war, Dreams of China

Chapter 2 The road to war, Dreams of China

Russo-Japanese War and rise of Japan
日露戦争と日本の台頭

 Serious trouble in the Japanese/American relationship began after the Russo-Japanese war (1904-1905). This war was a shock to the White Christian world. They had always assumed that White Christians would dominate the world as part of the natural order.
 Japan, being a non White, non Christian country, terrified them with their victory over Russia.

 日露戦争(1904〜1905)の後、日米関係に重要な問題が出てきました。この戦争は、キリスト教国の白人達にとって、とてもショックな出来事でした。何故なら、その白人の国々では、自分達が世界を支配する事が自然なこと、当然のことと考えていたからです。
 日本という国は、キリスト教ではない国、有色人種の国であり、この様な国が、白人キリスト教国であるロシアに戦争で勝利した事で、他の白人キリスト教国の人達は、日本という国をとても恐れるようになりました。

 America has always been a difficult society to enter. Americans always talk about how anybody can come to America and become American. For the Japanese person living in Japan, their only contact with America is some English teacher in Japan, they might easily believe that America is some wondrous country. Well in truth, in general, people in America do not kill immigrants. Most of the time. Yes, there are occasional riots, where immigrants do get killed.
 But most American immigrants come from war torn countries,

64

or a place where they are discriminated against as an ethnic or religious minority. And again in America, they face much prejudice. Their English is poor, their religion different, mostly they work at low level jobs, send their children to school, by the second or third generation they begin to achieve success in America.

　アメリカは、昔から入りづらい社会です。アメリカ人は大抵「誰でもアメリカに入国して、アメリカ人になる事が出来る」と言います。一般的な日本人は、アメリカ人というと、英語の先生に会う位しかないと思いますので、そういう話を聞けば、「ああ、アメリカは素晴らしい国だな！」と信じるかも知れません。確かに、アメリカ人は移民を殺すことはありません。ほとんど殺しません。ただ、たまに暴動が起こった時に、そこにいた移民が殺されることはあります。

　だいたいアメリカへ移民する人たちは、戦争中の荒廃した国から来るか、或いは差別を受けた少数派民族や宗教の人達がほとんどです。そしてまたアメリカで、移民に対する差別に沢山直面します。英語は上手くない、宗教は違う、その人達のほとんどは収入の低い仕事しか出来ません。だいたい、移民の2代目か3代目になると、アメリカ社会でも何とか成功出来ます。

Immigrants and discrimination
移民と差別

However until the Russo-Japanese war, most immigrants to America were white and Christian. It was after this period that many immigrants from Asia began to arrive, primarily from Japan and China. And right away Japanese people began to have friction with Americans. They worked too hard, more than

Chapter 2 The road to war, Dreams of China

established Americans. And the American reaction was to pass more restrictive laws.

　日露戦争の前のアメリカに移民する人達は、ほとんどが白人とキリスト教信者でした。その戦争後、アジアから、主に日本と中国からの移民が多くなりました。日本人の移民が増えると、早速、日本人とアメリカ人の間でトラブルが起こりました。それは、アメリカ人よりも日本人が一生懸命に働いていたためです。その為、アメリカ人の反動として、日本人の移民を排除するという法律を作りました。

This when extreme anti Japanese propaganda began to appear. There was "Letters of a Japanese schoolboy" by Wallace Irwin. This was the first appearance of the image of a Japanese person having buck teeth and round glasses. A similar character appeared in the movie "Breakfast at Tiffany's" where White American actor Mickey Rooney played "Mr. Yunioshi".

　この頃から、日本人に対してとても失礼なプロパガンダが溢れるようになりました。ウォレス・アーウィン作『日本少年の手紙』という本が有りました。この本から、出っ歯で丸メガネという日本人のイメージが作られたのです。有名な映画、『ティファニーで朝食を』の中で、その様なイメージの〝ユニオシさん〟という日本人キャラクターがいました。しかしこのキャラクターを演じた役者は、日本人やアジア人では無く、白人のミッキー・ルーニーという人でした。

This is a process that Itoh Kan in his book "Self extinction of the American Empire" calls "Demonization". Americans take some physical aspect of foreigners, or their names, and use this to mock people. This is why many new immigrants anglicize their names

第 2 章　戦争への道、中国に対する夢

Typical anti Japanese propaganda poster of the war era
戦争時代の代表的なプロパガンダです
出典左：Brainz.org「10 Most Xenophobic Pieces of Anti-Japanese Wartime Propaganda」右：cheezburger.com「Clint Gamboa Totally Looks Like Mr. Yunioshi」

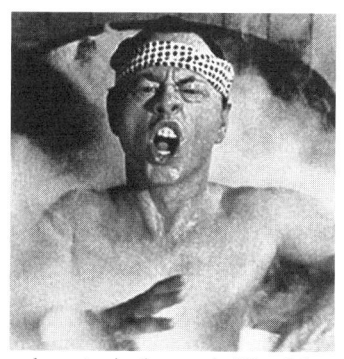

Mr. Yunioshi, a character in the movie "Breakfast at Tiffany's"
『ティファニーで朝食を』の映画のユニオシさんです
出典：Movieline「Breakfast at Tiffany's at 50: We Need to Talk About Mr. Yunioshi」

67

Chapter 2 The road to war, Dreams of China

when arriving in America. There is not much acceptance of non English names.

　伊藤貫氏はこのアメリカ人の差別について、彼の著書『自滅するアメリカ帝国』の中で、ディモナイゼーション（悪魔化）と呼んでいます。アメリカ人は外国人に対して、肉体的な事、或いは名前について、様々な側面から外国人をバカにします。アメリカに移民した人達が自分の名前を英語に直すのはこの為です。英語以外の名前はアメリカ人は受け入れないのです。

My own ancestor's dropped the "von" from our name when they arrived in the US. It was regarded as too German, not American. I made it a priority of mine to put it back when I was old enough.

　私の先祖は、アメリカに移民で入国した時に、私達の名字の〝フォン〟を外しました。彼らは、〝フォン〟はドイツ的な名前過ぎて、アメリカらしくないと考えていた為です。私は法律的に責任をとることが出来る歳になったら、すぐに自分の名字をドイツのままの〝フォン〟に戻しました。

Wallace Irwin also brought up the concept of Japanese infiltrating America and having sex with White Women. This has always been a fear of American White people. It was only after WWII that interracial marriage became legal in all the United States.

　ウォレス・アーウィンは、アメリカ人は日本人に対してこのような恐れを持っている、ということを書いていました。アメリカの白人男性が日本人男性を恐がっています。何故かというと、アメリカの白人男性の考えでは、日本人男性がアメリカへ移民してきている理由は、白人女性とセックスをする為で、白人女性を日本人男性にとられてしまうという不安がありました。昔から、白

第 2 章　戦争への道、中国に対する夢

人男性はこのような事にとても恐怖を持っています。異民族間の結婚がアメリカ全国で法律的に認められるようになったのは、第二次世界大戦後のことでした。

Before that time, It was a State by State affair. So a Japanese American couple could live openly in some states, but if they went to such a state forbidding interracial marriage, they would be arrested and put in prison.

The Hearst newspapers also printed many baseless rumors about dangerous Japanese. For example, a group of Japanese people establishing a cooperative fishing port on the Californian coast became a secret Imperial Navy base. Americans have never been a studious people, so it was easy for such rumors to spread.

Western men fear Japanese and White women
日本人に白人女性を奪われるというアメリカ人の恐れです
出典：Brainz.org「10 Most Xenophobic Pieces of Anti-Japanese Wartime Propagand」

Chapter 2 The road to war, Dreams of China

　Also Japanese people worked hard. The entire family worked hard, on the fishing boat or on the farm. Americans became angry at this.

　それまでは、州によって法律は違っていました。日本人とアメリカ人の夫婦はある州では生活に問題はありませんが、異民族間結婚が禁止されている州へ旅行したら、逮捕されて、刑務所に入れられました。

　ハースト新聞社も根拠の無い「日本が危険！」という噂の記事をたくさん書きました。例えば、カリフォルニアの海岸で、数人の日本人漁師が協同の漁港を造れば、ハースト新聞社では、これは日本帝国海軍の秘密基地であると書きました。アメリカ人は昔からあまり勉強しない国民ですから、その根拠のない噂は簡単に広がりました。

　それから、日本人は一生懸命に働いていました。農業でも、漁業でも、家族全員で一生懸命働いていたのです。アメリカ人はこのような勤勉さに対して怒りました。

Anti Japanese prejudice in America
アメリカの反日差別です
出典左：Densho: Japanese Internment during WWII
　　右：bookmice.net「Japanese-American Internment Camps」

第 2 章　戦争への道、中国に対する夢

I remember when I first came to Tokyo. I got a job at an English school. The secretary lived with her family near Ikebukuro. They had a Sushi restaurant. She worked there to help out. I asked her how much her father paid her, and she looked at me strangely. "Well of course I am not paid. It is the family restaurant." she replied. I was surprised. In a similar situation in America, family members would be paid.

Well, farm children in America help out with chores around the farm, without being paid. But in a shop situation, they would generally be paid.

　私が初めて東京へ来た時に、英会話学校で仕事をしていました。その学校の秘書は、家族で池袋の近くに住んでいて、家の商売は寿司屋だったのですが、彼女は英会話学校の仕事だけではなく、寿司屋でも手伝って働いていました。私がそのお手伝いには、お父さんからいくらお金をもらっているのかを彼女に尋ねると、彼女はの返事は、「勿論、お金は貰いません。家族の寿司屋ですから」。この答えにとても驚きました。アメリカでは、同じ様に家族の仕事を手伝ったとしたら、子供はお金を貰います。

　まあ、アメリカの農家の子供達はお金を貰わずに農場で働きますが、一般的にお店の場合は少しでもお金を渡すことが当たり前です。

I remember that after the Vietnam war, many South Vietnamese refugees came to the US. Of these, many who had been fishing people in Vietnam were settled on the US Gulf coast. The entire Vietnamese family would work on the fishing boat, which caused complaints from Americans. They said it was unfair competition.

　ベトナム戦争後、数多く南ベトナムからの難民がアメリカへ来たのですが、ベトナムで漁業を行なっていた人の多くは、アメリ

Chapter 2 The road to war, Dreams of China

カのメキシコ湾沿岸に定住しました。一隻の漁船でベトナム人家族全員が働いていることに、同じ場所で漁業を行なっているアメリカ人達が、不公平な競争であると怒り出しました。

 This resentment of Japanese hard work was part of the reason Japanese were declared by law an undesirable race in California in 1913. They were forbidden to buy land. I can see a lot of similarity between such laws, and the present TPP trade pact. Americans, instead of working harder themselves, try to use legal means to destroy other hard working races and peoples.

 1913年に、カリフォルニア州では、日本人は不快な民族であるから土地を買うことは出来ないという法律を作りましたが、本当の理由は、日本人の農民は一生懸命働き過ぎるので、自分達より良い農場を持ってしまうという恐れだったのでした。その昔の法律と現在のTPP貿易条約は同じ事でしょう。アメリカ人は自分で努力する事ではなく、法律を利用して、別の一生懸命働く人の努力を潰します。

 American prejudice and ridicule against Japanese immigrants was severe. While saying that they would welcome immigrants, and then abusing them and using them for their own profit, is a cold hearted policy. Because Japanese worked hard and saved money, this is the reason for Americans to hate them. This is the reality of America.

 アメリカの日本人移民に対する差別と嘲笑は酷いものでした。移民を受け入れると言いつつ、自分達の権益を奪うものにはとても冷淡でした。戦前の日本人移民は勤勉で財を築いたことが、アメリカ人による差別の原因だったのです。これらがアメリカの現実です。

Christianity and superiority
キリスト教と優位性

It was around this time, from 1913, that Christian missionaries began to seriously influence American policy towards Japan. Americans have always been deep believers in Christianity. However, the truth is, Americans pervert the religion. They use Christianity to justify American superiority, and dominance of other nations.

There is nothing in Christianity that declares any nation, including America, be superior and have the right to dominate other nations. But that is how Americans choose to interpret the Bible.

1913年頃から、アメリカのキリスト教宣教師達が、日本に対するアメリカの政策に大きく影響を与えるようになりました。アメリカ人は昔からキリスト教を深く信じています。しかし、真実はアメリカ人はキリスト教を曲解しています。アメリカ人は自分達が他国の支配をすること、アメリカが上位であるという気持ち、それらをキリスト教を利用して正当化しているのです。

キリスト教の教えの中には、アメリカを含めてどんな国でも、どの国が上位であるとか、他国を支配する権利があるとは書いてありません。しかし、アメリカ人は自分達に都合が良いように聖書を解釈しています。

In 1911, China had a nationalist revolution led by the leaders such as Sun Yat-sen, who developed the Three Principles of the People. It was very difficult, and in 1913, the new revolutionary Chinese government asked Protestant Christian churches around

Chapter 2 The road to war, Dreams of China

the world to pray for their success. This greatly pleased the Americans.

It pandered to their ego of being a master country. They began to feel that they should protect China.

1911 年に、三民主義を唱えた孫文を中心に中国で国家主義革命（辛亥革命）が起こりましたが、その新しい中国政府は問題が山積みでしたので、1913 年に、その新しい中国の革命政府は世界中のプロテスタントのキリスト教会に自分達の革命の成功を祈るよう要求しました。この要求はアメリカ人をとても喜ばせました。

自分達が「世界を支配する国である」という考えに迎合したのだと。それから徐々に、アメリカ人は中国を守らなければならないという気持ちになって行きました。

Christian missionary boards across the country began to preach the virtues of China. Americans believed that China would become a Christian nation, that would be obedient to America, and carry out America's wishes. There were some 26 mission boards across America. They reached the mass of American people, presenting a good image of China.

There were a few Japan societies in the cities, but they could only appeal to American elites. They just could not compete with the power of the mission boards in presenting a good image of Japan.

アメリカの全国の宣教師団は、徐々に中国が素晴らしい国であると説教するようになりました。アメリカ人は、そのうち中国はキリスト教国に改宗するに違いない、アメリカに従順でアメリカの望みを実現してくれると信じていたのです。アメリカ全国で 26 の宣教師団がありました。宣教師達は多くのアメリカ人に影響が有り、中国の良いイメージを多くの人々に与えたのでした。

大都市にはいくつかの日本協会（Japan societies）が有り、ア

第2章　戦争への道、中国に対する夢

メリカのエリート層には影響を与える事が出来ましたが、アメリカ人に日本の良いイメージを伝えるために障害になる、宣教師団と競争出来ませんでした。

Also at the time, President Wilson was a devout Christian. He was born in Virginia in the American South. In such a state, views that the White race had the right to rule non White races were unquestioned.

So President Wilson began to take a very negative view of Japan, and a very positive view of China.I think that in the mind of President Wilson, Japan, a non White, non Christian nation, was seen to challenging the natural order of White domination. The Chinese were very smart to use America in this way.

当時のウィルソン大統領は敬虔なキリスト教信者でした。アメ

President Wilson
ウィルソン大統領
出典："Woodrow Wilson (Nobel 1919)" bby A. B. Lagrelius & Westphal, Stockholm パブリックドメイン

Chapter 2 The road to war, Dreams of China

リカ南部バージニア州で生まれましたが、その州は、白人は白人以外の民族を支配する権利を神様から受けている、という愚かな考えが特に強い所です。

それで、ウィルソン大統領は徐々に日本が悪で、中国が良い、という見方をするようになりました。ウィルソン大統領は、日本という非白人で非キリスト教国が、白人支配が当たり前の自然の法則に挑戦をしていると考えるようになりました。この様にアメリカを利用して、やっぱり中国人は頭がいいですね。

Such feelings about Japan are still true today in America. In discussing WWII with Americans, they say that Japan needed to be punished for WWII because Japan started an aggressive war. Well, Americans ignore the fact that they provoked Japan into attacking Pearl Harbor, that America had it's own Empire in Asia. They also remain mute about attacking Iraq and other countries.

And another point. The American missionaries did not have all that much actual great success in China. But they desperately wanted to believe so. In recent times, Chinese authorities have harshly clamped down on religions like Christianity and Tibetan Buddhism, and new religions like the Falun Gong. I do not think they would have allowed a foreign religion like Christianity to gain any real influence.

現在のアメリカでも、このような見方はまだ強く根付いています。アメリカ人と大東亜戦争の事を話すと、彼らはたいてい、日本が攻撃をして戦争を始めたから、日本を罰する必要が有ったと言います。そう、アメリカがアジアで自分の帝国を持っていたことや、アメリカが、日本が戦争を引き起こす様に扇動したこと、この事実をアメリカ人は無視します。イラクをはじめ、他の国へのアメリカの攻撃も無視します。

もう一つ重要な事があります。本当のところは、アメリカの宣

教師達は中国では大してキリスト教に改宗させる事が出来なかったのです。しかし、アメリカの宣教師達は、多くの中国人をキリスト教に改宗出来ると信じたかったのです。最近では、中国政府は、キリスト教やチベット仏教を弾圧し、また法輪功等の新宗教に対して厳しく弾圧しています。やはり、キリスト教のような外国の宗教を、中国で布教させて広めることは中国政府が許さなかったでしょう。

Demonization of Japan
日本の悪魔化イメージ作り

In the First World War (1914-1918), Japan and America were allies. This fact is ignored in American high schools, at least it was not taught in history where I went to high school. Americans just do not want to admit that Japan has positive aspects. This is a process called demonization.

Actually, looking at World War One, I don't think any side could really be called "good" or "bad". There were opposing sides, caused by friction between powerful countries. Of course, in English speaking countries, Imperial Germany is portrayed as "bad", because America and Great Britain fought them. So in the American mind, America was "good" to fight "bad" Imperial Germany in World War One.

第一次世界大戦（1914年〜1918年）で、日本とアメリカは同じ連合国でしたが、この事実は、アメリカの高等学校では無視されています。少なくとも私の高等学校で教えられませんでした。アメリカ人は、日本に肯定的な面が有る事を認めたくないのです。この方法は、ディモナイゼーション（悪魔化）と呼ばれています。

実際に、第一次世界大戦を考えると、どちら側が〝良い〟、ど

Chapter 2 The road to war, Dreams of China

ちら側が〝悪い〟と言うことは出来ません。原因は、強力な国同士のぶつかり合いだからです。勿論、英語圏の国では、米英がドイツ帝国と戦いましたから、ドイツ帝国は〝悪い〟と描写されています。それで、アメリカ人の考え方では、第一次世界大戦でアメリカは〝悪い〟ドイツと戦った〝良い〟国でした。

Since America does not trust Japan, the fact that Japan was an ally against Imperial Germany is an inconvenient fact. Thusly, it is not mentioned. Such activity, such as demonizing Japan, is

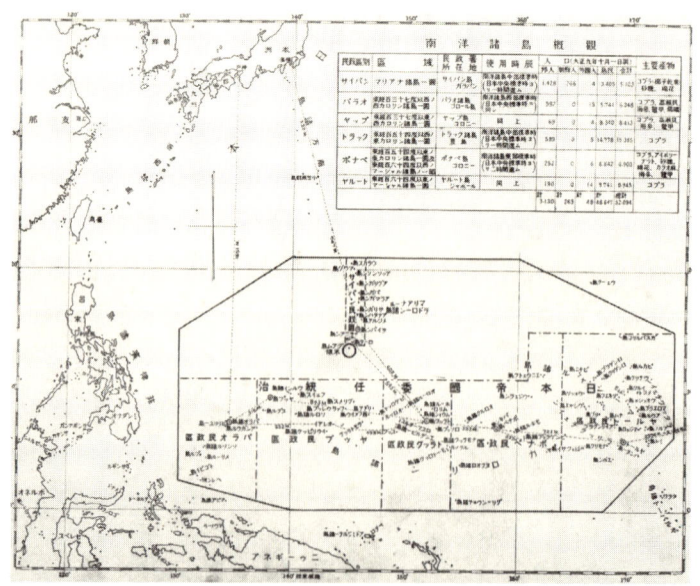

The post WWI Japanese Pacific Mandate
第一次世界大戦後、日本が委任統治した南洋諸島（囲みの中）です
（囲みの中央左の小さな円が米領グアム、囲みの外西側が米領フィリピン）
出典：『南洋群島写真帖：日本帝国委任統治』海軍省編 -1922

not done by any type of government regulation or order. It is the cultural consciousness of the American people themselves.

After this war, Japan received a mandate from the League of Nations to rule former German island possessions in the Central Pacific. This greatly alarmed American leaders. The Japanese mandate surrounded the American possession of Guam, and was directly across sea communications to the Philippines.

American Hearst newspapers stepped up their propaganda on how Japan was a threat. Japanese immigrants into the US were dangerous, Japan would invade China, Japan would build secret Naval bases in Mexico. These were the kinds of articles printed. They created a poisonous atmosphere in the US, it became very difficult to say anything positive about Japan.

　アメリカは日本を信用しないので、日本が同じ連合国としてドイツ帝国と戦った事は都合の悪い事実です。だからこのことには言及しません。このような日本に対しての、ディモナイゼーションはアメリカ政府の命令では無く、アメリカ国民の文化的な意識が元にありました。

　第一次大戦後、日本は国際連盟から中央太平洋にある元ドイツの植民地だった島々の委任統治を託されました。これにより、アメリカの指導者達は危険性を感じ、日本を警戒しました。この日本の南洋庁はアメリカ所有の植民地グアムを囲って、フィリピンとアメリカとの繋がりをブロックしていると。

　ハースト新聞社は「日本が危険である」というプロパガンダを強化し、増やしました。アメリカへの日本人移民が危険である、日本は間もなく中国を侵略するだろう、メキシコに日本が海軍の秘密基地を造っている。この様な記事をばらまくことで、アメリカ国内に日本は有毒な国であるという雰囲気を作りだして、日本について肯定的な話をすることが出来なくなりました。

Chapter 2 The road to war, Dreams of China

At the Paris Peace Conference of 1919, American President Wilson felt a responsibility to protect China from Japan. Why? Americans like foreign countries to be weak and needing American help. This feeds the American ego, that America is the best country and culture in the world.

Also, as I have written, America has always had a dream of China. They just look at the numbers of Chinese people, and imagine all those people buying American products. The truth here is, I don't think Chinese would really buy American products. OK, Coca Cola is a world brand. But the kind of goods America made in the 1920's were hardly suitable for a country like China.

1919年のパリ講和会議で、アメリカのウィルソン大統領は中国を日本から守る責任感を感じていました。何故でしょうか？　それは、アメリカ人は、弱い国、アメリカの支援が必要な国が好きです。支援する事で、アメリカは世界一の国である、アメリカの文化が世界一であるという自尊心を満たしてくれるからです。

昔からアメリカ人は中国への夢を持ってきました。中国の人口の多さを考えると、その人口の多い中国人が皆アメリカ製品を買い、とても儲かるという事を想像してしまうのです。実際には、中国人はアメリカ製品をそれ程買わないでしょう。確かにコカコーラは世界的なブランドです。しかし、1920年代にアメリカが造った製品は、当時の中国には合わなかったのです。

And having experience with American businessmen in Japan, they do not study or research what might sell in another country. They simply expect other countries to buy their products as is.

Some years ago, I was in a company that introduced an American ice cream franchise into Japan. What they did was take a cut section of ice cream, mix in fruit flavors, nuts, cookies, and so forth according to the customers order. I went to their main office

第 2 章　戦争への道、中国に対する夢

in the center of the United States to study their operation. Right away, I found a serious problem.

　私は、日本でアメリカ人ビジネスマンと仕事をした事があります。彼らは他国で物が売れる為に、勉強、研究をしません。自分が造った製品をそのまま他国で売れると思っています。

　何年か前に、アメリカのアイスクリームのフランチャイズを日本に紹介する会社で働きました。その会社では、アイスクリームのある部分を取り分けて、果実の味、ナッツ、クッキー等、お客様の注文によって様々なものを入れました。その会社の方針を学ぶ為にアメリカの本社へ行きました。そしてすぐに、大きな問題に気がつきました。

The ice cream was made in tubes of cardboard. The store worker, usually a high school student, would then cut the ice cream, while still in the tube. I said to the American company officials, "Well, some of the cardboard must remain in the ice-cream when it is cut?" Their reply was, "Only a little". I told them that for Japanese people, food purity is very important. Any piece of cardboard in an ice cream order would be a major problem.

The Americans just could not comprehend this. They could not understand why Japanese have different standards than Americans. After 6 months of negotiations, we finally settled on using plastic, that would not remain in the product when cut.

　アイスクリームを厚紙のチューブで造っていたのです。アルバイトの人は大抵高校生で、厚紙のチューブに入っているアイスクリームを切ります。アメリカの社員に、「切る時にアイスクリームに厚紙が残るでしょう？」と質問をしたところ、彼らの返事は、「少しだけ」でした。私は日本で食料品の販売をするには、清潔であ

81

Chapter 2 The road to war, Dreams of China

る事はとても重要であることを教えました。不潔に厚紙が残っているアイスクリームを販売するという事は、日本では大変な問題になると。

そのアメリカの社員は、この事を理解出来なかったのです、日本人はアメリカ人と基準が違うという事実を。半年間交渉の後、やっとアイスクリームに残らないプラスチックを使うことを決めました。

In the 1919 Paris Peace Conference, Japan wanted a phrase added into the treaty to end racial discrimination. American President Wilson refused. Well, he was from Virginia, a southern state. But in general, White Americans don't like racial equality.

That is true even in modern times. They will say they believe in racial equality, but they don't practice it. Too many Japanese people simply believe what Americans say. You have to observe what Americans actually do to see the truth.

先述のパリ講和会議で、日本政府は人種差別をなくす文言を条約に入れたいと考え提案しましたが、アメリカのウィルソン大統領が拒否し認められませんでした。まあ、彼はアメリカ・バージニア州出身で、南部でしたから特にかもしれませんが、基本的に、アメリカの白人は人種平等が嫌いです。

これは現在にも当てはまる真実です。アメリカ人は人種差別の無い社会が有ると言いますが、実際には差別の深い社会が有ります。アメリカ人の言う事を簡単に信じる日本人が多過ぎます。真実を理解する為には、アメリカ人の行動を観察しなければなりません。

第2章　戦争への道、中国に対する夢

Conquering the Philippines
フィリピン征服

I have written here that the American military was upset about Japan acquiring former German islands in the Central Pacific ocean. Japan's new area of control lay athwart the sea communication routes to the Philippines.

Well, what about the Philippines? America went to war in 1898 to free the Cubans and Philippine people from oppressive Spanish rule. Well this is what the Hearst newspapers said. That was a lie. After the war, America dominated every Cuban government until the revolution of Fidel Castro in 1959.

In the Philippines, the Philippine revolutionary leaders were outraged that after destroying Spanish forces, America decided to conquer the Philippines as a colony for itself. The result was a ten year war, in which 200,000 to 1,500,000 Philippine civilians were killed.

　私は、第一次世界大戦の後、日本が元ドイツ植民地の島を取得することになった事に、アメリカ軍が怒り動揺したと書いています。日本の南洋庁が置かれた新しい地域は、アメリカのフィリピンへの海の通信経路を横切っていました。

　さて、フィリピンはどのような問題でしたでしょうか？　1898年に、アメリカはキューバとフィリピンを圧政的なスペインの支配から解放する為に戦争を始めました。まあこれは、ハースト新聞が書いたことです。これは嘘でした。その米西戦争の後、アメリカは1959年のフィデル・カストロの革命まで、全てのキューバ政府を威圧し支配しました。

　フィリピンでは、アメリカがスペイン軍を潰してから、アメリカが自国の植民地としてフィリピンを征服するつもりであるとい

Chapter 2 The road to war, Dreams of China

う真実を知り、フィリピン革命のリーダー達は憤慨しました。その結果は 10 年間の戦争で、20 万人から 150 万人のフィリピンの民間人が殺されました。

  Mark Twain was a vocal critic of this war. But you won't find the Philippine-American war, or Mark Twain's criticism, being taught in many American schools. Americans hide inconvenient truths. Actually, many Americans themselves were not enthusiastic about conquering the Philippines. There is a phrase in American English, "America is The Reluctant Empire". I agree, Empire does not suit America.

  Of course the American missionaries complained about Japan loudly. They felt that Japan was too strong against China. Japan for it's part did make some gestures to China. Most favored nation status was offered. But China at the time was too chaotic to respond.

　作家のマーク・トウェイン氏はこの戦争を強く批判しました。しかし、アメリカの多くの学校では、この戦争について、或いはマーク・トウェイン氏の批判について教えません。アメリカ人は不都合な真実を隠します。実際のところ、アメリカ国民はフィリピンを征服することについてあまり前向きではありませんでした。アメリカ英語に「アメリカは不承の（嫌々引き受けた）帝国です」というフレーズが有ります。私は同意します。帝国的な事はアメリカに合いません。

　勿論、アメリカの宣教師は強く日本の事を批判していました。日本は中国に対して強過ぎると思っていました。実際には、日本は中国との交渉を試みていました。最恵国待遇での交渉もしましたが、中国国内は混乱し過ぎていて、返事をすることが出来ませんでした。

第2章 戦争への道、中国に対する夢

Two reasons for the Japan-U.S. war
日米戦争の2つの理由

And here are the two major events that caused Japan and America to have a war. The American colonization of the Philippines, and the Christian missionaries desire to convert all of China to American Christianity.

The reader might notice that I don't have any personal commentary in the last few pages. The reason is simple. Even today, the reasons Japan went to war are too dangerous to discuss with Americans.

ここに日本とアメリカが戦争に至った二つの理由が有ります。それは、アメリカのフィリピン植民地化と、アメリカのキリスト教宣教師が中国をキリスト教に改宗することを望んでいたことです。

この本の読者の方は、私がここ数ページ、個人的な意見を書いていないということにお気づきかもしれません。その理由は簡単です。現在でも、アメリカと日本が戦争を始めた理由を、アメリカ人とはっきりと議論する事は危険過ぎるのです。

Many Japanese people have a very fantasyland type idea of America. They think that in America, you automatically get freedom, and the right to speak and do as you please. Not at all. There are many rules and restrictions. There have to be. In Japan, there is a social common sense. Because Japan has a long history and culture, people intuitively know how to behave.

American history is about 1/10 of Japan's. There has been no time to develop such a cultural common sense. And America

Chapter 2 The road to war, Dreams of China

is a land of immigrants. Each group has differing ideas of how a society should function. So in order to avoid chaos, America needs strong laws, and strong police to enforce them.

　日本人の多くは、アメリカという国に対して幻想を抱いています。アメリカでは、皆自動的に自由を得られ、好きな話、好きな行動が出来ると思っています。全然違います。ルールと制限が多

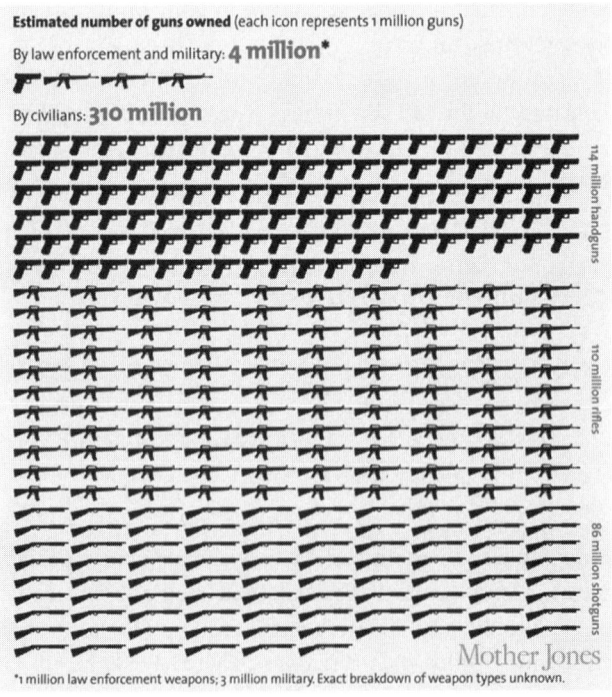

Estimated number of guns owned (each icon represents 1 million guns)
By law enforcement and military: **4 million***
By civilians: **310 million**

114 million handguns
110 million rifles
86 million shotguns

Mother Jones
*1 million law enforcement weapons; 3 million military. Exact breakdown of weapon types unknown.

Comparing private gun ownership (below:310 million) to the police and military (above:4 million)
アメリカの軍隊・警察が持っている銃の数（上部：400万本）と、一般のアメリカ人が持っている銃の数（下部：3億1千万本）の比較チャートです
出典：『Mother Jones』2013年1月31日付「10 Pro-Gun Myths, Shot Down」

86

いのです。それらが必要なのです。日本では社会の常識が有ります。日本は長い歴史と文化が有りますから、人々は正しい行為を直感的に分かっています。

　アメリカの歴史は日本の10分の1です。その社会に合う常識を醸成する時間が無かったですし、アメリカは移民の国です。各民族毎に社会的行動については違う考え方が有ります。その為、社会が混乱に陥らない様に、アメリカには強い法律、強い警察が必要なのです。

When I was young and lived in America, I feared policemen. That is common sense in the USA. If you get involved with a policeman, it is involving serious trouble, somebody could get killed. To be fair, most Americans have guns. So a policeman or woman, seeing a problem, he or she never knows if they will be killed.

There are people who intentionally start fights to attract the police. When the police come, they kill them. That is why in most cities, there are certain neighborhoods where police will not answer calls, it is too dangerous.

　私が若い頃に、アメリカに住んでいた時、警察官が現れると怖かったです。アメリカでは、それは当たり前です。アメリカで警察官と関係するのは重要なトラブルですし、人が殺されるかも知れないことです。公平を期すため、警察官の立場から言うと、ほとんどのアメリカ人が銃を持っています。ですから、事件が有れば、警察官は自分自身が殺されるかも知れません。

　時々、警察を呼び込む為に敢えて問題を起こす人がいます。そして、警察官が来ると、殺してしまうのです。罠です。そのため、アメリカの各大都市には、非常に危険なため警察官が通報に応えない地域が有ります。

Chapter 2 The road to war, Dreams of China

  Years ago when I was single and lived in New York City, I had an argument with my date on the street. Suddenly the police were there. I stopped, stood still, and slowly put both hands out in front of me. This was to show the police I had no weapons. This is common sense behavior in America. If you move too quickly, they may shoot you.

  In my situation, the police already had their hands on their guns. With me, they realized I was giving them control, they relaxed with me. My date started screaming at the police, that was the end of our relationship.

  When I first came to Japan, I was also afraid of Japanese police. Simply because in America it is dangerous to be near police. But I gradually learned that Japanese police are very helpful, not at all dangerous to average people.

  何年か前、私が独身でニューヨーク市に住んでいた時に、恋人と通りで言い争いをしました。突然、周りに警察官が集まっていました。私は動きを止めて、ゆっくり両手を私の前に出しました。これで、私は警察に武器を持っていないことを示します。アメリカでこのような行動は常識です。急に動くと、警察から撃たれる可能性が高いです。

  私の場合、その時警察官はもう拳銃を手にしていました。そして私の出している手を見て、私が警察官に逆らう意思がないことが分かりました。私がデートしていた彼女は警察官に叫び出し、それで私との関係が終わりました。

  私は初めて日本に来た時に、日本の警察を恐れていました。何故なら、アメリカでは警察官の近くに居る事は危険だからです。しかし、徐々に日本の警察官は人を助ける存在で、一般の人にとって危険な存在では無いという事が分かりました。

  America is a country of constant violence and struggle. You

第2章　戦争への道、中国に対する夢

have to constantly fight to maintain your position. And Americans believe they are the greatest people in the world, every other country is inferior to them. So if I would try to explain the true course of Japanese/American relations before the Pacific war, it would naturally involve a screaming argument, or even possibly a fist fight.

It takes incredible patience to discuss something with an American, and often it is impossible. Just last fall, I read in the Huffington Post electronic newspaper, instructions on how to win arguments with relatives at holiday dinners.

In November, there is Thanksgiving, and Christmas is in December. Many family members gather for the holiday dinner. And alcohol is there. It seems that there are so many family arguments, the Huffington Post, gave instructions on how to argue about topics such as Obamacare. Other very controversial topics are Global Warming, or religion.

　アメリカは永遠に暴力と闘争の国です。自分の地位を守るために、いつも闘わなければなりません。アメリカ人は自分達が世界一素晴らしい国であり、世界の他の国々は自分達より劣っていると信じています。だから、もしも私が大東亜戦争前の日米関係の真実を説明しようと試みたら、それは怒鳴りあうような議論、或いは拳で戦うことになるかも知れません。

　アメリカ人と議論する為には、本当に忍耐が必要ですが、それでも議論にならない場合が多いです。この前の秋に、ハフィントンポスト電子新聞に、アメリカの祭日に食事をしている時の、親戚との議論の勝ち方を教えるという記事が有りました。

　11月は感謝祭、12月にクリスマスがありますので、家族の皆が食事で集まります。そこにはお酒もあるでしょう。やはり家族同士での言い争いが多く、ハフィントンポストは色々なトピック、例えばオバマケアを議論する方法を説明していました。その他に

Chapter 2 The road to war, Dreams of China

特に論争となるトピックは、地球温暖化や宗教についてです。

So you can just imagine how I would do at an American holiday dinner, if I came up and said "American President Roosevelt goaded Japan, until Japan launched the attack at Pearl Harbor. He knew it was coming, and deliberately sacrificed old second class warships."

That is fact of course. But there would be a lot of screaming. And of course if I tried to discuss the Comfort Women issue, or Nanking, and to explain that Japan is not truly an evil nation, and that America has it's own nasty history, well, my host family would ask me to leave.

この事を想像して下さい。私がどこかのアメリカの家族に感謝祭の食事に招待されたとします。そこで、私が「アメリカのルーズベルト大統領は、日本が真珠湾攻撃を行なうまで、日本を扇動しました。そして真珠湾攻撃が行なわれる事を知っていながら、敢えて古い２級戦艦数隻を犠牲にしました！」と言ったとします。

勿論、これは真実です。でも、アメリカ人とこのような話をすると、怒鳴られます。それから、慰安婦問題、南京事件などを説明しようとしたり、日本は本当に悪の国ではないと言ったり、アメリカも悪い事を行なった事が有るという話をしたら、その家族は「帰ってくれ！」と言います。

As a child, I always thought in WWII that it was strange that America was so emotional about China. China is very far away from America. And why did America take over the Philippines? As a child, these questions puzzled me.

For Japan, events in China were vital. They were right next door to Japan itself. In this sense, I can understand why Japan invaded

第 2 章 戦争への道、中国に対する夢

China. China was chaotic, falling into internal disarray. Foreign powers were cutting out their own shares of China. If China became under foreign domination, Japan itself would be in danger.

　私は子供の時にアメリカで育ちながら、第二次世界大戦の時に、アメリカ人が何故こんなに中国について感情的だったのか不思議に思っていました。中国はアメリカからとても遠いです。そして何故アメリカがフィリピンを征服したのか？　この問題で当惑していました。

　日本の場合、隣の国なので、中国国内の状態は日本国にとって非常に重要でした。この部分で、日本が中国大陸に進んだ理由が分かります。中国国内の状態は、白人、キリスト教の強い国々が中国を自国の植民地として分割していましたので大混乱していました。もし中国が外国に支配された場合、日本は危険だったからです。

Well Americans do the same thing. There is the Monroe doctrine. This states that no European power may interfere in Central or South America. The area is America's to control. America forced a war with Mexico in 1846. All through the 1920's American Marines fought in various Central American countries. These wars were called the "Banana Wars", because they were often fought on behalf of American fruit companies. One of the United States Marine Corps most famous officers, Major General Smedley Butler, made a famous statement, "War is a racket" concerning this period.

　アメリカ人も同じ事をします。モンロー主義という宣言が有りました。アメリカはこの宣言で、ヨーロッパの国は、中央アメリカ・南アメリカには手を出すなと命令しています。この地域はアメリカが支配している場所です。1846年にアメリカが一方的にメキシ

コ戦争を始めました。1920年代、アメリカ海兵隊は中央アメリカの様々な国々で戦いました。そのほとんどがアメリカの果物会社の為に戦ったので、これらの戦争は〝バナナ戦争〟と呼ばれました。アメリカの海兵隊の有名な士官、スメドレー・バトラー中将は、この時代について、「戦争は詐欺である（多数の犠牲の上にごく少数の資本家が莫大な富を得る詐欺である）」という有名な発言をしました。

So, we have increasing anti Japanese feeling in America, a colony in the Philippines that is near Japan, and Christian missionaries throughout American society who feel that America must protect China from Japan.

そして、アメリカで反日の気持ちが高まっていたため、アメリカ社会の中では、日本の近くにあるアメリカの植民地フィリピンと中国を、日本から守らなければならないという考えを持っているキリスト教宣教師が数多く居ました。

Three Americans in charge
３人のアメリカ人戦争責任者

Now let us look at three people who helped push Japan and America into war. If I was to choose any one person with the greatest responsibility, I would choose Henry L. Stimson, who was greatly aided in his quest for war by President Franklin Roosevelt and Secretary of State Cordell Hull.

さて、これから、日米戦争開始に関してアメリカ人の、３人の責任者を考えてみましょう。誰が最も戦争責任があるか、一人を選ぶなら、ヘンリー・スティムソン氏を選びます。ルーズベルト大統領とコーデル・ハル国務長官は戦争への作戦、道を探るのに、

第 2 章 戦争への道、中国に対する夢

彼にとても助けられたからです。

 Henry Stimson had served as governor of the Philippines. That experience left him with several strong beliefs. This was the superiority of American protestant Christianity and the superiority of the White race. He believed that his two year term as Governor of the Philippines taught him everything that he needed to know about Asian people. This was a strong belief that Asian people need guidance from White people, and that White people should be strict with them.

 Since Japan was an independent non White nation with a strong military, it was natural that Henry Stimson would have extreme dislike for Japan. He constantly engaged in intrigue to try to bring the United States and Japan to war. He is responsible for Japan

Henry Stimson
ヘンリー・スティムソン
出典：Library of Congress 所蔵　Harris & Ewing bw photo portrait（1929 年）

Chapter 2 The road to war, Dreams of China

leaving The League of Nations.

　ヘンリー・スティムソン氏は植民地フィリピンの元総督でした。この経験で彼はいくつかの強い信念を持ちました。それは、基本的に、アメリカのキリスト教のプロテスタントと白色人種が世界では上位であるという優越性です。彼は、自分のフィリピン総督の経験で、アジア人の色々な民族を全て理解することが出来たと信じていました。当時、白人の国では、アジア人は白人からの指導と厳しい扱いが必要である、という深い信念がありました。

　日本は強い軍隊を持っている独立したアジアの国でしたので、ヘンリー・スティムソン氏が持つ日本に対する嫌悪感は当たり前でした。彼はいつも日米戦争になる様に陰謀を画策していました。日本が国際連盟を脱退した事は彼の責任であると言えます。

 He created a secret letter, which was read in the League of Nations assembly. The letter accused Japan of being an immoral nation. Japan being a proud nation, walked out. In American history books, this walkout is portrayed as proof that Japan was a nasty country. In those history books, there is no mention of Mr. Stimson's provocations.

 As Secretary of State under President Hoover, and as Secretary of War under President Roosevelt, Henry Stimson worked hard to portray Japan as an evil nation to American elites. And he succeeded. There was no other person in America who understood Japan, or could explain what Japan needed to survive.

　彼は、日本は不道徳な国であると非難する秘密の手紙を書きました。そしてその手紙は国際連盟の議会で読まれたのです。誇りを持っている国、日本は国連を脱退しました。現在でも、アメリカの歴史教科書で、この脱退は日本が悪い国である証拠として教えられています。その歴史教科書にヘンリー・スティムソン氏の

陰謀の手紙が原因であるということは書いていません。

　彼はフーヴァー大統領の下で国務長官、日米開戦時のルーズベルト大統領の下で陸軍長官で、彼は一生懸命、アメリカのエリートに日本が悪い国であるというイメージを植え付ける為の努力をしました。彼は成功しました。そしてアメリカには、日本を理解している、或いは日本が生存する為に何が必要かを説明出来るアメリカ人は居ませんでした。

President Roosevelt had a strong affection for the American Navy. So it was only natural that he would regard the Japanese Imperial Navy as a rival. Also, his mother had lived in China, and had told him many romantic stories about China as a child.
And Cordell Hull had felt from a young age that Japan should be restrained.

　ルーズベルト大統領はアメリカ海軍に対して深い愛情を持って

President Roosevelt (left) and Cordell Hull
ルーズベルト大統領（左）とコーデル・ハル国務長官
出典左：Library of Congress 所蔵　Elias Goldensky（1933 年）／
　　右：Library of Congress 所蔵　Chicago Daily News（1924 年）

Chapter 2 The road to war, Dreams of China

いましたので、日本帝国海軍をライバルと考える事は当然のことです。彼の母親は、中国に住んでいた事もあり、彼が子供の頃に、中国についてのロマンチックな話をよく話し聞かせていました。コーデル・ハル氏は若い頃から、日本を抑えるべきであるとの気持ちが有りました。

Interventionist Americans
干渉するアメリカ人

Americans are a very interventionist people. This is both as a nation, and as individuals. They always believe that their own opinion is correct, and everybody should change their ways and follow American opinions.

アメリカ人はとてもよく干渉する国民です。これは国としてでも個人としてでもそうです。自分の意見は正しいと信じて、世界の人々が自分と同じ意見、やり方、に変えるべきであると信じています。

I remember as a young man, it was my dream to join the US Marines. I went to high school in a small town in America.   For my initial physical examination, I had to travel to a military hospital in the city of Milwaukee.

I went by Greyhound bus. Many Japanese people always tell me how friendly Americans are. Well, it is true that people easily begin a conversation with strangers, but that does not always mean friendly.

The person sitting next to me on the bus began a conversation with me. Of course, he asked where I was going. When I said that it was my desire to join the military, and I was on my way for a physical examination, the passenger next to me suddenly became angry. Very angry.　You see, this was the time of the Vietnam war, and that war polarized American society.　You had to be for, or against the war. If you do not have a strong opinion one way or the other, people treated you like a fool. I felt at that time that it was my duty to join the military.

　私の若い頃の夢は、米海兵隊に入る事でした。私はアメリカの小さな町の高校に行ったので、まず一番始めの身体検査の為にミルウォーキー市の軍病院へ行きました。

　私はそこまでグレイハウンドバスで行きました。日本人から、アメリカ人はとても友好的だということをよく聞きます。まあ、知らない人と簡単に会話を始める事は本当ですけれど、それはいつも友好的であるという意味では有りません。

　バスで私の隣に座っている人は私と会話を始めました。私がどこへ行くのかという事も聞いてきました。私は軍隊に入る為に身体検査をしに行くと返事をすると、その人は突然怒りました。とても怒り出したのでした。当時はベトナム戦争の時代でしたが、その戦争でアメリカ社会は分極化していたのです。当時、アメリカ人は戦争反対、或いは賛成のどちらかでした。曖昧な意見は周りの人々から許されませんでした。その時、私は軍隊に入る事は国の為の義務と感じていました。

This person began to scream at me that I was a terrible person for wanting to join the military.　He said that it was my desire to kill innocent women and children in Vietnam.　Well in my heart I also got angry.　This was a bus trip, we happened by chance to sit next to each other.　I did not know his name.　Yet this person felt he had the right to tell me how to live my life.　In general, I have found it best to avoid deep conversations with Americans.

Chapter 2 The road to war, Dreams of China

This is what Americans are. In this era, I feel that the Vietnam war was a terrible American mistake. It was mistake just like provoking Japan into attacking Pearl Harbor was a mistake. America today is using similar methods to push TPP. I understand that there is a lot of screaming by the American delegates at Japanese delegates to do things the American way.

このバスで隣に座っている人は叫び始めました。例えば、私のことを、こいつはひどい人間だ、こいつの希望はベトナムへ行って、罪無き女性、子供を殺す事だ！と。私は心の中で怒りました。これはバスの旅で、彼は偶然隣に座っただけで、彼の名前も知りませんでした。しかしこの人は、私に、人生をどう生きるべきか言う権利が有ると思っていました。基本的に、私はアメリカ人とは深い話を避けます。

アメリカ人とはこういう人々です。現在、私はベトナム戦争は恐ろしいアメリカの間違いだと思っています。日本を真珠湾攻撃に扇動した事と同じ様な、恐ろしい間違いだと思っています。アメリカは現在でも同じ様なやり方でTPPを押しつけています。私が聞いた話では、会議の中でアメリカ代表はいつも日本代表に向かって叫んでいるそうです。

In Japan, people do not push their opinions upon others, people try to coexist peacefully. Japanese people do indeed persuade other people to do things the Japanese way. But the method is very different. I remember some years ago, a friend owned several restaurants. One of them was a small Thai restaurant. There were many problems. For example, if the Thai manager did not feel like working, he would not open the restaurant.

日本では、人は他人に自分の意見を押し付けるような事をしないで、平和的に共存する事を努力しています。日本人も確かに日

第２章　戦争への道、中国に対する夢

本人の様なやり方をするよう他国人を説得します。しかし、方法は全然違います。数年前にある友達はいくつかのレストランを所有していました。その中の一つは、小さなタイレストランでした。そこには多くの問題が有りました。例えば、ある日そのタイ人マネージャーが、仕事をやる気が無いので、レストランをオープンしないということがありました。

Well, I like Thailand and Thai people very much. But I have to admit that in Thailand, they have a very easy going attitude towards work, very unlike Japanese people. So what the Japanese owner did, he began to spend most of everyday at that Thai restaurant. Often, he would miss his last train home. He slept on the chairs in the restaurant after closing. By his hard work, he demonstrated to the Thai manager how to manage a restaurant in Japan.

And he was successful. The Thai manager changed his work habits, today that restaurant is expanding, one of the best in Tokyo. I really think that Americans should learn workplace management from Japanese people. And they should cease so much military intervention in other countries.

　私はタイ国とタイ人が大好きです。しかし、タイ人は仕事に対してのんきな気持ちが有る事は真実です。日本人と違います。その為、日本人オーナーはだんだんその問題のタイレストランに来て、そこで過ごす時間がとても増えました。何回も終電に間に合わないこともありました。そんな時はレストランの営業が終わってから、椅子の上に寝ていました。自分が一生懸命に働くことで、そのタイ人マネージャーに日本の仕事のやり方を教えました。

　それは見事に成功しました。現在、そのレストランは増えていて、東京のタイレストランの中でもわりといいお店です。私は本当に、アメリカ人は日本人から経営を学ぶべきだと思います。そ

99

Chapter 2 The road to war, Dreams of China

して、アメリカ人の干渉方法が戦争を生んできた現実を直視すべきです。

China, an invading nation
侵略する中国

There is a propaganda film from the war period, "Why We Fight". It portrays Chinese as a very peace loving people. There was a statement in the beginning of the film, "China has never invaded anybody". This is designed to make Japan look like a monstrous country for invading such a peace loving China. The facts are, China has always been a violent land. As far as never invading any country before WWII, a quick google check shows at least 22 invasions of Vietnam.

当時のプロパガンダ映画に『何故戦うのか』が有ります。この映画では、中国人はとても平和的な国民であると描いています。映画の始まりに有る言葉は、「中国は決して他国を侵略した事が有りません」。これは、とても平和的な中国を攻撃した、日本が恐ろしい国である、と見せるために作られています。真実は、中国は昔から暴力的な国です。ちょっとグーグルで検索しただけでも、中国は22回ベトナムに侵略した事が有ります。

Not to mention many very nasty civil wars. China also had the custom of publicly executing people in a gruesome fashion. There was a torture, "Death by Thousand Cuts". A person would be stripped naked, and tied to a pole in a public square, before all the people. Then Chinese officials would slowly cut pieces of their body off. It could take several hours to die. That China has deep

100

history and culture is of course quite true. But there is also the brutal side.

　中国はとてもひどい内乱がよく起こりましたし、中国の公開死刑は本当に残酷でした。凌遅刑という拷問が有りました。死刑人は裸にされて、公共の広場で柱に縛られます。そして、中国の公務員が少しずつ死刑人の体から肉の部分を切ります。死刑人が死ぬまでに数時間かかることもありました。中国は長い歴史、素晴らしい文化があった事は勿論真実です。でも、残酷な側面も有りました。

At the time of WWII, it was the dream of American leaders that China would become America's junior partner in Asia, and police Asia for American profit. One more thing that angered me about that film "Why We Fight", was the bit about Japanese air raids on Shanghai. There is that famous staged photo of the crying baby sitting in the ruins after the Japanese air attack.

The commentator mentions how terrible Japanese forces were to kill women and children. Well, in a war, women and children die. Shanghai was a battlefield. But the Japanese Imperial Armed forces did not deliberately target women and children. They can also be combatants, a woman or a child can use a weapon or carry a bomb. This is sad fact.

But the movie commentator put a moral tone to his speech. Yet, at the same time, American bombers were firebombing Japanese cities, which were full of women and children. This is another ghastly aspect of the American character. They accuse other people of being terrible, when they themselves do the same thing. America attempted to exterminate the Japanese people by bombing. They killed something like 1,500,000 people at least.

Chapter 2 The road to war, Dreams of China

　第二次世界大戦の時に、アメリカのリーダー達の夢は、中国がアメリカのジュニア・パートナーとなり、アメリカの利益の為にアジアを管理するということでした。このプロパガンダ映画『何故戦うのか』のもう一つの事に対して私はとても怒っています。それは、上海空襲の事です。日本軍による空襲後の焦土に泣いている赤ちゃんが座っているという、故意に効果を狙ってアレンジされた有名な写真が有ります。

　映画のコメンテーターは、女性と子供を殺していた日本軍が酷いと言っています。残念ながら、戦争で女性と子供も死にます。上海は戦場でした。しかし、帝国陸海軍は意図的に女性と子供を殺そうとはしませんでした。女性と子供も戦場で戦う場合も有ります。武器を使用したり、爆弾を運ぶ事も出来ます。悲しい真実です。

　この映画で、日本が酷いと言っているアメリカ人コメンテーターは道徳的な言葉を使っています。しかし、アメリカの爆撃機は、女性や子供が多く存在している日本の都市を空襲しています。これは、アメリカ人の性格の恐ろしい側面です。別の国の人が悪い事をしていると告発しますが、実は自分達も同じ事を行なっているのです。アメリカは日本国民を空襲で絶滅しようとしました。少なくとも、150万人位殺しました。

It was easy for Americans to feel that they must save China. And the government of Chiang Kai Shek understood this and used it to receive American help. But he had no intention of ever becoming a servant of America. This is what Americans just could not understand. In the modern era, it seems that Americans regard China as an enemy. Well, in part. What Americans want is a weak China that will obey American wishes. They have no use for a strong China that could take an independent course. And Americans feel the same way about Japan.

第2章　戦争への道、中国に対する夢

　アメリカ人が中国を援助する必要があるという考えを持たせる事は簡単なことでした。蒋介石政権はその事を十分理解して、アメリカの援助を受ける為に利用しました。しかし、彼はアメリカの手下になるつもりは絶対に有りませんでした。アメリカ人はこの事を理解していませんでした。現在は、アメリカは中国を敵国として考えているようです。それは、半分は本当のことです。アメリカ人の希望は、アメリカに従う弱い中国です。強い、自分の独立した道を作れる中国は敵とみなします。そして、アメリカ人は日本に対しても同じ気持ちを持っています。

　There are many of my friends in Japan who think that President Hoover might not have started a war with Japan. Well certainly, he had a more non interventionist view. There were some Americans who understood Japan's advance into China, as a defense against Communism.
　There were people in the State Department, who also understood that China was not actually pro American. These State Department people issued a report saying so in 1935, but a protege of Stimson, Stanley K. Hornbeck, buried the report until 1938. The hardliners won out in portraying Japan as an evil nation.

　多くの私の日本の友人は、フーヴァー大統領は日本との戦争を始めていないと考えています。確かに、彼は日本に対して干渉的な立場ではありませんでした。何人かのアメリカ人は日本の中国大陸での行動は、共産主義から日本を防衛する為であることを理解していました。
　それはアメリカの国務省の中の人々で、彼らの中には中国はアメリカ向きの国ではないという事を理解している人も居ました。その国務省の人たちは、そのようにまとめた報告書を1935年に作成しました。しかし、スティムソンの後輩、スタンリー・クー

103

Chapter 2 The road to war, Dreams of China

ル・ホーンベック氏が、1938年までこの報告書を隠していたのです。日本が悪い国であるというイメージを作り上げた強硬路線の人たちの勝利でした。

It was Stimson who pushed to put economic pressure on Japan over French Indochina. He felt that it was American pressure that forced Japan to withdraw from Siberia in 1922. Here again, we have an example of American simplistic thinking.

When Japan allied with Germany and Italy, Americans feared invasion by both Japan and Germany. I have seen maps in Life magazine from the period, showing how Germany and Japan could attack the US. These were very fanciful assumptions, actually ridiculous.

Germany did not have a big surface Navy, Germany could not even invade England. It was impossible for the Japanese Navy to mount an invasion across the Pacific.

スティムソンはフランス領インドシナの問題で日本への経済制裁を進めました。彼は、1922年の日本のシベリア撤退はアメリカの外圧の影響であると考えていました。これはやはりアメリカ人の単純な考え方です。

日本がドイツとイタリアと同盟を組んだ時に、アメリカ人はドイツと日本、両国からの侵略を恐れていました。私は当時のライフ雑誌の地図を見た事が有ります。その地図で、日本とドイツがアメリカ大陸を侵略するルートを示していましたが、それはとても空想的な仮定で、本当に愚かな記事でした。

ドイツの海軍は水上艦の数が少なく、英国にも侵略することは出来ませんでした。そして日本帝国海軍は太平洋を渡ってアメリカ大陸を侵略する事は絶対に不可能でした。

第 2 章　戦争への道、中国に対する夢

8 point plan to force Japan to start a war
日本に戦争を始めさせる 8 つの計画

So the US government came up with an 8 point plan to force Japan to start a war. This was very important for American planners. If Japan started the war, American provocations would go unnoticed.

それで、アメリカ政府が日本から戦争を始めさせる為の、8つの計画を考えました（海軍情報部極東課長のアーサー・H・マッカラム海軍少佐が作成した「マッカラムの戦争挑発行動 8 項目覚書」参考文献 236 ページ参照）。これはアメリカ人にはとても大切なことでした。もし日本が先に攻撃を始めれば、将来、アメリカが仕掛けた日本に対する扇動であることが分からないだろうからです。

The steps taken to force Japan to war were:

この戦争を促す計画の実行ステップは次の通り：

1) An agreement was reached where America would have the ability to use British Naval ports, in particular Singapore, and in the Dutch East Indies.
1）アメリカが英国の軍港、特にシンガポールの使用について英国との協定締結する。

2) An agreement was reached where America would have the ability to use base facilities and acquisition of supplies in the Dutch East Indies.
2）オランダ領東インドに有る基地を利用出来る協定をオランダと結ぶ事。

Chapter 2 The road to war, Dreams of China

3) Support China's Chaing Kai Shek as much as possible.
3) 中国の蒋介石政府を出来るだけ援助する事。

4) Sending US cruisers on "pop up" cruises in the Western Pacific. To FDR's thinking, to start a war, he was willing to lose 1 or 2 cruisers. For example, on July 31st, 1941, off the Imperial Naval base at Sukumo in Shikoku, two blacked out cruisers suddenly appeared. When challenged by Japanese destroyers, the ships fled.
4) 東洋にアメリカ海軍巡洋艦艦隊を派遣する事（この巡洋艦の使命は日本の領海に浸入することでした。F・ルーズベルト大統領の考えは、戦争開始の為には、1隻か2隻を失うことも問題ないというものでした。例えば、1941年7月31日に四国の宿毛沖で国籍不明の巡洋艦2隻が突然現れ、日本帝国海軍の駆逐艦2隻を挑発して逃げました）

5) Increasing the number of American submarines based in the Pacific.
5) 太平洋の基地にアメリカ海軍の潜水艦を増やす事。

6) The permanent basing of the Pacific fleet in Hawaii.
6) 太平洋艦隊をハワイに配属する事。

7) Forbidding the sale of oil to Japan from the Dutch East Indies.
7) オランダ領東インドから日本へ石油の販売を禁止する事。

8) Forbidding the sale of oil to Japan from America.
8) アメリカから日本へ石油の販売を禁止する事。

Now, you just can not discuss this subject with most Americans. I remember when I was a child, I calculated that the US fleet at

Pearl Harbor was merely bait. The newest US battleships were on the East Coast, where there was no danger from Germany. The carriers were pulled out at the last minute.

When I discussed my idea with my father, I got punched in the face. He screamed at me that no US government would sacrifice US sailors. Actually, that is not true.

In fact, in his book "Day of Deceit: The Truth About FDR and Pearl Harbor" Robert Stinnett describes how US Naval Intelligence tracked the Japanese Pearl Harbor attack fleet on their way to Hawaii. If you mention this book to Americans, they get very angry, and claim the entire book is a falsehood.

　アメリカ人とこの真実のことは、話をすることが出来ません。私が子供の頃、真珠湾のアメリカ艦隊は只の〝囮〟と推測していた事を覚えています。一番新しいアメリカの戦艦は東海岸に有りましたので、ドイツからの危険性は有りませんでした。そしてハワイから航空母艦はぎりぎりで撤退されていました。

　この考えを父親に話をすると、彼は私の顔を殴り、アメリカ政府がアメリカの水兵を犠牲にするはずがないだろ！と怒鳴りました。実際には、それは本当の事では有りません。

　『デイズ・オブ・ディシート（邦題：真珠湾の真実 ― ルーズベルト欺瞞の日々）』という本で、ロバート・スティネット氏は、アメリカ海軍情報部局は真珠湾を攻撃する日本の艦隊を、択捉からハワイまでの移動を追跡して把握していたと書いています。この本の事をアメリカ人と話をすると、とても怒り、すべて嘘であると叫びます。

Most Americans truly like war. I used to belong to a forum on the net called "Historic Battles". It was a forum to discuss military history. Well, very quickly, I became very controversial. I argued that Japan had just cause to go to war. The Europeans

Chapter 2 The road to war, Dreams of China

would consider my views, but the Americans became very angry with me.

Then it was 2003 and America prepared to invade Iraq. I warned that it would be a disaster. The Americans on the forum howled that I should be banned from posting. Well, the moderators were European, so I was not banned.

One Jewish American fellow in New York claimed to have Israeli friends in Tokyo who could kill me. Because I was against the American desire for war. The moderators got angry at that.

アメリカ人は本当に戦争が好きです。数年前に、「歴史的に有名な戦争」というネットフォーラムで、昔の戦争を議論しました。すぐに物議を醸し論争になりました。私は大東亜戦争は日本が戦争を開始する理由が有った、という主張でした。ヨーロッパ人は私の主張を考え検討しましたが、アメリカ人はすぐに怒りました。

2003年、アメリカは徐々にイラクに侵略する為の準備をしました。私はアメリカがイラクを侵略したら、大惨事になるだろうと警告しました。そのフォーラムのアメリカ人メンバーは、私を参加禁止にしよう！と叫びました。まあ、モデレーターたちはヨーロッパ人でしたから、私は参加禁止にはなりませんでしたが。

あるニューヨーク市に住んでいるユダヤ系アメリカ人が、東京にイスラエル人の友達がいると書いて、彼らに私を殺す依頼をすると書きました。何故なら、私はアメリカ人の戦争を始めたいという欲望に反対したためです。その脅しに対してフォーラムのモデレーターたちは怒りました。

Well of course, the war did turn out to be a disaster. President Obama was forced to leave Iraq, under threat of more guerrilla war. He did try hard to stay. Americans left in the middle of the night, without telling their Iraqi counterparts.

And yes, there were some American commentators and pundits

who were against the war. Mostly, they lost their jobs. And those who cheer leaded the war, who said it would be a cakewalk? Mostly they are in think tanks, with a nice income.

There was a plan to destroy Japanese society. Even today, America seeks to dominate Japan.

勿論、その戦争は大惨事でした。オバマ大統領は撤退するしかありませんでした。もし撤退しなかったら、イラク人がまだゲリラ戦をアメリカに仕掛ける脅威が有りましたので。結局同盟のイラク軍に黙って、米軍は夜逃げをしました。

アメリカでは、イラク戦争反対の評論家、コメンテーターがいましたが、現在、ほとんどの人は職を失いました。それでは、その戦争を応援した評論家とコメンテーターは現在どうなっているかというと、ほとんどの人は良い収入が有り、シンクタンクで働いています。

もし、アメリカには日本に戦争を仕掛けさせる８つのステップがあった、と言ったらアメリカ社会からは抹殺されるでしょう。今でもこれは危険な議論なのです。

Was there a way to prevent the war?
戦争を避ける方法はありましたか？

Was the The Pacific War inevitable? Did Japan have no choice but to attack America? Many Japanese friends ask me this. They feel that if Japan and America had made some kind of compromise, war could have been avoided.

I don't think so. In general, in American society, to compromise is to be regarded as weak. Americans admire strong people. The meaning of this is that strong people force others to bend to their will.

Chapter 2 The road to war, Dreams of China

In Japan, compromise is regard as necessary for everyday life. In the 40 years I have lived in this country, I have seen many Americans struggle with this. Americans demand their rights, and are used to being forceful to get them. This is why on a personal level, most Americans don't work out well in Japanese society.

　大東亜戦争は避けることが出来なかったのでしょうか？　本当に、日本はアメリカに攻撃する選択しか無かったのでしょうか？
　多くの日本人の友達から、こういう事を私は聞かれます。もし日本が何とか妥協したら、戦争を避ける事が出来たはずでしょうと。
　私はそう思いません。一般的に、アメリカ社会では妥協する事は弱い人とみなされます。アメリカ人は強い人を称賛します。この意味は、強い人が強制的に弱い人を自分の意向に従わせるということです。
　日本では、日常生活の為に妥協が必要と考えます。私は約40年間日本に住んで、多くのアメリカ人はこの考え方を理解することが難しい様に見えます。アメリカ人はいつも自分の権利を要求しています。この理由で、個人主義的な、ほとんどのアメリカ人は日本社会での生活が難しいでしょう。

We must understand the mindset of President Roosevelt, Cordell Hull, and Henry Stimson did not want peace with Japan. They wanted war, and they wanted Japan to start it.
 Japan did propose several compromises, such as partial withdrawal from Indochina according to "A Republic, Not an Empire: Reclaiming America's Destiny" by Patrick J. Bucahanan. America refused. If Japan had accepted American demands, Japan would have ceased to exist as an independent nation.
 Japanese people are a very kind hearted people. They just cannot imagine that some other country or person could have bad

第 2 章　戦争への道、中国に対する夢

intentions. Well, to Americans, their intentions were not bad. They feel it is natural that America should dominate the world. They cannot, and do not want to understand that such domination brings immense suffering to other people. Americans will never treat another country as an equal.

　私達は、ルーズベルト大統領、ヘンリー・スティムソン氏、コーデル・ハル国務長官の考え方を理解しなければなりません。彼らは日本との平和を望んでいませんでした。どうしても戦争を始めたい彼らの望みは、日本から戦争を開始する事でした。
　実は、日本はいくつかの妥協を提案しています。例えば、フランス領インドシナから部分的な撤退です（参考文献 238 ページ参照）。しかし、アメリカが拒否しました。もしも日本がアメリカの要求を受け入れたら、独立国家としての日本は終わっていたでしょう。
　基本的に、日本人は心優しい人々です。他人、他国が悪意を持って接してくるという事を想像出来ません。アメリカ人の場合、自分の日本に対しての考えは悪く無いと思っています。アメリカが世界を支配する事が当たり前だと思っています。その支配が、他国の国民にとても苦しみを与えるという事を理解したくありませんし、理解することは不可能です。アメリカ人は絶対どんな国でも平等な扱いをしません。

So really, the Japanese military had no choice but to fight. And the strategy of the Japanese military was reasonable. Japan could not invade and destroy America. But the strategy of gaining island territory as a buffer was the only possible one. And it nearly worked. I will write more about this in the next chapter.

But, is it true that there was nothing that Japan could have done to prevent war? I can think of one possibility. Japanese leaders of the time understood the expansionist and domineering mindset of Americans. But they did not understand how to appeal to

Chapter 2 The road to war, Dreams of China

Americans in a positive way.

Americans are a very emotional people. They really don't understand facts. Recently, in an article on the electronic newspaper "Huffington Post", I read an article that 25% of Americans believe that the sun orbits the earth.

本当に日本帝国軍は戦う選択しか有りませんでした。それと、日本の帝国軍の戦略は合理的でした。日本はアメリカに侵略して、崩壊させる事は不可能でした。しかし、いくつかの島をアメリカ攻撃の緩衝地としてとる戦略は、唯一可能な戦略でした。そして、ほとんど成功しました。その事を次のチャプターで書きます。

しかし、本当に、日本は戦争を避ける方法が何もなかったのでしょうか？一つの可能性が考えられます。当時の日本の指導者はアメリカの拡張主義、横暴で支配的な考え方を理解していました。しかし、アメリカ人に主張する方法を理解していなかったのです。

アメリカ人はとても感情的な国民です。真実を本当に理解出来ません。最近、ハフィントンポスト電子新聞では、アメリカ人の25％が太陽が地球の軌道に乗って周っていると信じていると報じています。

Japanese spirit was the core of the post war prosperity and power
日本精神が戦後の日本の繁栄と力の中心に

The Chinese government of Chiang Kai Shek understood that by giving Americans the idea that they could Christianize China, he would get American help. He got more than that, America forced Japan into a war that would destroy Japanese military power. But Chiang Kai Shek never ever truly thought of letting American Christianity have any real influence in China. If that had ever

第 2 章　戦争への道、中国に対する夢

appeared possible, he would have simply killed every Christian.

What Japan might have done is appeal to America that Japan was a true Democracy, while China was not. It would have taken a lot of work. But Americans perceived Japanese society at the time of being a dictatorship. No it wasn't. Even so, I think in 1941 it would have extremely difficult to convince Americans that Japan was a reasonable country.

中国の蒋介石政権は、アメリカ人に中国をキリスト教国に改宗する事が出来ると思わせて、アメリカからの援助を受けました。中国はもっと素晴らしい援助を受けました。アメリカが日本の軍事力を潰す戦争を扇動したことです。しかし、勿論、蒋介石氏はアメリカのキリスト教が中国で実際に影響を与えるような活動は許しませんでした。もしそれが可能になるようでしたら、中国のキリスト教信者は絶滅させられたでしょう。

日本がアメリカに、日本は本当の民主主義国であること、中国とは違うという事を主張したら良かったかも知れません。けれど、それは大変難しかったです。当時、アメリカ人は日本を独裁主義の国であると思っていました。それは真実とは違いました。それでも、1941 年にアメリカに対して日本は合理的な国である、ということを納得させる事は多分無理だったでしょう。

In 1941, if Japan had fully given in to American demands, it would have been the equivalent of a military surrender. America would have certainly occupied Japan with it's military, the Japanese Imperial Army and Navy would have been disbanded. Japanese industry would have been destroyed. Japanese people would have been forced to work in American corporations for American profit. At a slave like existence. Japan would have become like any other European colony.

Japanese leaders knew that the chance of victory was slim. But

113

Chapter 2 The road to war, Dreams of China

by fighting so courageously, the Imperial Japanese Army and Navy bought Japan time. Even though Japan lost the war, America was shocked by the tenacity of the Japanese military. Even though America did occupy a defeated Japan, Japanese industry was preserved. America could not totally destroy Japan. This was to be the core of Japanese post war prosperity and power. For this, millions of Japanese soldiers, sailors, and civilians sacrificed their lives.

　1941年に、もし日本がアメリカの要求をすべて受け入れたら、軍事的な降伏と同じことでした。アメリカ軍が日本を占拠して、帝国陸海軍は解散させられていたでしょう。日本の産業は破壊されていたでしょう。そしてアメリカの利益の為に、日本人は強制的にアメリカ企業で働かされ、奴隷のような存在になっていたはずです。日本は他のヨーロッパの植民地と同じ状態になっていたでしょう。

　日本の指導者達は勝利の可能性は低いと分かっていました。でも、非常に勇敢に戦って帝国陸海軍は時間を稼ぎました。日本は戦争に負けても、日本帝国軍の不屈で粘り強いことにアメリカはショックを受けました。アメリカの負けです。日本を占拠しても、日本の産業は残され、アメリカが日本を完全に潰す事は出来ませんでした。この精神が戦後の日本の繁栄と力の中心になりました。その為に、兵士、水兵、一般国民が、命を犠牲にしたのです。

Korea uses the United States
アメリカを利用する韓国

In the present age, we have a similar problem. Koreans are mounting a world wide campaign to discredit Japan. In particular, they are using the issue of Comfort Women in WWII to portray Japan as an evil nation. This is a brilliant tactic. In America, the concept of Feminism is very strong. American women cannot accept at all that prostitution can be in any way voluntary.

And Americans naturally like to be seen as helping people. Koreans are using these American traits to attack Japan through the United States. Frankly, most of the things they say are complete lies. Koreans were enthusiastic Japanese citizens at the time.

Americans don't know these facts, and don't care. When Koreans come to Americans and say, "We are poor oppressed victims of Japan", Americans will believe them unconditionally.

現在の日本は、その当時と似ている問題が有ります。韓国人は、世界的に日本を悪い国であるように見せる宣伝活動を行なっています。特に、慰安婦問題を日本が悪い国であると見せる為に利用しています。これは見事な作戦です。アメリカではフェミニズムがとても強いですから、アメリカの女性は売春行為が自発的に行なわれたという事を理解しません。

それから、アメリカ人は人を助けている事を自慢する事が好きです。韓国人はこのアメリカ人の国民性を利用して、日本に攻撃しています。正直に言うと、韓国人が言っている事はほとんど嘘です。当時、韓国人は熱狂的な日本国民でした。

アメリカ人はこの真実を知らないし、興味が有りません。韓国人がアメリカ人に、「私たちは日本に虐げられてきた可哀想な犠牲

Chapter 2 The road to war, Dreams of China

者です」と言うと、アメリカ人は簡単に信じます。

But the truth is that many women were unknowingly sold by their parents, or were deceived by a broker selling women, and were thus brought into the industry against their will. So the evil party here is that broker (most of them were Koreans), or the girl's parents. It was not the Japanese Army, or the Japanese government, that forced these girls into prostitution.

At the present time, the Japanese government is making no response to these world wide Korean activities. And Japanese/American relations are rapidly deteriorating. I think in Japan, a grass roots effort by Japanese people is the only way to avoid serious trouble.

　中には、知らないうちに親に売られていたり、女衒の甘言に騙された人もいて、それは本人の意思に反していたでしょう。それはその人の親や悪い業者（多くが朝鮮人）の責任であり、強制したのは日本軍や政府ではないということです。
　現在の日本政府はこの韓国人の世界的な行動に対して、反論、対応をしていません。そのせいで、日米関係は急激に悪くなっています。私は日本が、この深刻な問題を避ける方法は、一般国民の草の根の努力しかないと思います。

In this battle Japanese women will be very important. I know many Japanese women who are very angry about the Korean fabrications about the Comfort Women issue. Perhaps we should invite some prominent American feminists to Japan for a conference with Japanese women activists. And if the government won't help, perhaps Japanese corporations could help fund this.

After all, I think Koreans will soon begin suing Japanese corporations in America in American courts to pay compensation

116

for the Comfort Women. If we do nothing, Japan will be damaged.

　この戦いで、日本人女性はとても重要で大切な存在です。私は韓国の嘘に対して怒っている多くの日本人女性を知っています。例えば、アメリカの有名なフェミニストを、日本人女性と討論する為に、招待する事が良いかも知れません。日本政府が動かない場合は、日本企業が手助けすると良いのではないでしょうか。
おそらく、韓国人はそのうち在米日本企業に対して、アメリカの裁判所で告訴して、戦争時代の慰安婦への補償を要求するでしょう。このまま何もしないと、日本はますます損害を受けます。

第 3 章　大東亜戦争

Chapter 3　The Pacific War

Chapter 3 The Pacific War

The truth about the Japanese military
日本帝国陸海軍の真実

Until now in this book, I have written a basically chronological record of events between Japan and America. The reason for that is, I wanted to show how American mistakes and misunderstandings led to war. Instead, I will focus on various things that are constantly demeaned in American propaganda.

For example, did Japan's leadership selfishly force Japanese people into war? Were the Imperial Army and Navy truly brutal organizations?

When I first came to Japan 40 years ago, I realized that the truth of the war was not being discussed in Japan, it was hidden. I knew that this would be problem some day.   I will address such questions in this chapter.

　この本では、基本的に年代にあわせて日本とアメリカの交流の歴史を書いています。その理由は、アメリカの誤解と間違いが日米戦争への道へと導いたということを示しておきたかったからです。　これから、ちょっと違う方向からのことを書きます。大東亜戦争の戦いの話は様々な本に細かく書かれていますので、その本で読んで下さい。代わりに、これからアメリカのプロパガンダで、いつも品位を落とされている日本の大東亜戦争における活動に集中して書きたいと思います。

　例えば、日本の指導者達が自分達の欲の為に日本国民を強制的に戦争の道へ引っ張りましたか？　日本帝国陸海軍は本当に残虐、残忍な組織でしたか？

　私は40年前に初めて日本へ来た時に、大東亜戦争の真実は日本社会では話題にならず、隠されているとすぐに気付きました。私は、これはいつか、将来的に問題になるであろうと考えていま

した。このチャプターではそのような問題について述べます。

So Japan attacked the American Naval base at Pearl Harbor on December 8th 1941. December 7th for the Americans. Right away, Americans began calling it a sneak attack, a stab in the back.

In America, there is the concept of the fair fight, front to front. To stab someone in the back with a knife is not regarded as fair. Americans say that, but they behave otherwise.

When I first came to Japan, I was amazed to find Japanese people who believed that Japan was bad for attacking before the declaration of war had been issued. Why? When Japan attacked the Russian fleet at Port Arthur without a declaration of war in 1904, Americans cheered.

さて、1941年12月8日に日本が真珠湾軍港を攻撃しました。アメリカでは12月7日です。すぐにアメリカ人からこれは奇襲攻撃と呼ばれ、背中からナイフで刺す事だと言われました。

アメリカでは、公正な戦いは面と向かって戦うことという哲学が有ります。背中からナイフで刺すとは狡いという意味です。アメリカ人はそう言いますが、自分達の行動は違います。

私が日本に初めて来た時に、宣戦布告の前に攻撃したのだから、日本が悪いと信じている日本人に会って、驚きました。日本人なのに何故そう考えるのですか？ 最初私は、この手の日本人を理解出来ませんでした。アメリカ人が戦う時に宣戦布告はあまり意味が有りません。2003年にアメリカがイラクに攻撃した時は、宣戦布告をしていないのにアメリカは爆弾を落とし進軍しました。1904年の日露戦争では、日本が宣戦布告無しで旅順港のロシア艦隊を攻撃した時に、アメリカ人からは歓呼の声が上がりました。

Chapter 3 The Pacific War

If Americans do something to other people, they don't care. If something is done to them, then they scream and yell like a demon has appeared. This propaganda was words of the enemy. At the time, America was an enemy of Japan, of course they will not say anything complimentary about Japan. American propaganda engaged in demonization of Japan right from the start of the war. Japanese aircrew were quite superior to Americans at the beginning of the war. Japanese trained harder, and they had war experience.

　アメリカ人は他国民に対して何かをする場合は気にしません。その代わり自分が何かされた場合は、悪魔が出たかのように叫びます。その当時のプロパガンダは敵の言葉です。当時、アメリカは日本の敵でした。勿論、日本について敬意をはらうような話はしません。 アメリカのプロパガンダでは戦争の開始から、日本のディモナイゼーション＝悪魔化が行なわれました。戦争開始当時、アメリカより日本の航空機乗組員は優れていました。アメリカより一生懸命訓練を受けていましたし、戦争経験も有りました。

On the other hand, there was the story of how Japanese aircraft were inferior because they soon caught fire. Not at all. Japanese aircraft had extreme long range. So they were built lightly to fly far. It was amazing that the range of the Zero fighter was twice as long as Amerian aircraft at first. American aircraft were heavily armored, so they could not fly far. But they did not catch fire easily.

　一方、日本軍機には簡単に火がつくことが分かり、日本軍機は劣っているというプロパガンダがなされました。しかし、それは全くもって間違いです。日本軍機は長距離を飛ぶために設計されていたので、その理由で軽量化して造っていたのです。特にゼロ

戦の飛行距離は驚異的で当初アメリカ機の２倍ありました。アメリカ軍機は装甲が厚く、重い為、長距離を飛べなかったのですが、簡単に火はつきませんでした。

The propaganda coming out of America quickly turned very racial. A lot of Western commentators have long said that Japan's war against America was hopeless. That there was no way that Japan could have won. Not at all. Japanese strategy was the best that could be done. Japanese leaders understood that Japan had no chance to invade America and force it's submission. So it was decided to take some island chains and use them as a buffer against the American counter attack.

And it very nearly worked. Americans were shocked at the casualties in attacking the island of Tarawa. As the war went on, Americans tired of the long casualty lists. It was necessary for the American government to keep it's propaganda machine running full time to get people to support the war. In Clint Eastwood's movie, "Flags of our fathers" we can see how this propaganda campaign was run.

アメリカのプロパガンダはすぐにとても民族差別的なものになりました。数多くの西洋人コメンテーターは、日本はアメリカと戦争する事が無謀で、勝利の可能性はなかった、と言っています。そんな事は有りません。日本の戦略は考えられる中で最高のものでした。日本の指導者達は、アメリカ大陸に侵略して、アメリカを降伏をさせる事は不可能であるということを理解していました。ですから、いくつかの群島を取って、アメリカへ反撃の緩衝として使うことにしていたのです。

そして、その戦略的な計画はかなり成功に近いところまで行きました。アメリカ国民はタラワの戦いで多くの米兵が死んだことに、とても衝撃を受けていたので、アメリカ政府は、アメリカ国

Chapter 3 The Pacific War

民が戦争を支持するよう仕向ける為に、継続的にプロパガンダを作る必要に迫られていました。クリント・イーストウッド氏の映画、『父親たちの星条旗』で、このプロパガンダの活動を確認することが出来ます。

Japanese strategy was very similar to the strategy of the Confederate States of America in the American Civil War. Both nations had the same goals, they simply wanted to be left alone. Well, why did America win? The answer is very simple. Material. America had more of everything. During the war, Japan built only a few Fleet carriers, the Taiho with 83 aircraft, and three Unryu class carriers of 63 aircraft. America built 24 Essex class with 100 aircraft each.

This statistic alone shows how American production

The aircraft carrier Akagi
航空母艦赤城
出典：Japanese Navy　パブリックドメイン

overwhelmed Japan. It was not the technical gap but the material that was decisive, for example, American steel production was 60 times that of Japan. Personally, I think the average Japanese infantry man in The Pacific War to be greatly superior to the American soldier. In general, when American troops landed on an island, the Japanese defenders knew that there was really no hope of Japan being able to save them. They fought until wiped out. Americans could not understand such fighting. To Americans, there was no dishonor in surrender when a battle was lost.

　日本の戦略はアメリカ南北戦争のアメリカ連合国と非常に似ていました。アメリカ連合国と日本帝国は同じ目標を持っていて、どちらの場合もその時の独立した状態を保ち続けることでした。それでは、どうしてアメリカが勝ったのですか？　その質問の答えは簡単です。軍需資材です。どんな物でも、アメリカは全て日本より数が有りました。戦争中、日本はわずか数隻の大型航空母艦、大鳳（航空機83機を搭載）と３隻の雲龍型（航空機63機を搭載）、アメリカはエセックス級航空母艦24隻、そして各エセックス級は軍機100機が有りました。

　この統計の値だけでも、アメリカの生産力が日本を圧倒していたという事がよく分かります。科学技術力の差ではなく圧倒的な鉄鋼等の物質差（60倍）によって日本は負けているのです。個人的には、平均的に日本の歩兵はアメリカ兵よりとても優れていたと思っています。基本的に、アメリカ軍がどこかの島に上陸すると、守っている日本兵には日本から援軍が来る望みは有りませんでした。日本軍は絶滅まで戦いました。アメリカ人はこの様な戦い方を理解することは出来ません。アメリカ人の考えでは、負けが決まっている戦いの場合、降伏する事は不名誉ではありません。

　To compare, when Japan attacked Corregidor island in 1942, the American command surrendered in one day. When American

Chapter 3 The Pacific War

recaptured the island in 1945, it took ten days to retake it. Japan's last ground victory in the war was on Okinawa in April of 1945. The resistance in the south was so fierce that the US Army gave up, and had to be relived by US Marines. Some Ameircans have asked me why Japan did not simply surrender, when it was obvious that America would continue to advance.

　例えば、1942年に日本軍がコレヒドール島を攻撃した時のことと比較すると、アメリカ軍は1日で降伏しましたが、1945年のアメリカの反撃の時、日本軍を破るまで10日かかりました。アメリカ軍に対する日本帝国陸軍の最後の陸上戦の勝利は、1945年4月の沖縄戦でした。沖縄本島の南部における日本帝国陸軍の戦いは熾烈を極め、アメリカ陸軍は戦うことを諦めて、海兵隊に交代した程でした。 何人かのアメリカ人から私は、アメリカ軍を退かせることが出来ない事が明らかな状況で、どうして日本はもっと早く降伏しなかったのか？と訊かれました。

 I think one such serious reason was president Roosevelt's demand for unconditional surrender. Such a statement means that Japan would cease to exist. America might simply kill all Japanese people, or enslave them. Americans always tell me such fears were nonsense, Japan should have surrendered. But if we consider the Japanese viewpoint, it was difficult to trust Americans. Before the war, America always tried to diplomatically damage Japan.

 And if you read John Dower's book, "War without Mercy", half of the Japanese soldiers who tried to surrender to Americans were killed outright. A scene like this was shown in Clint Eastwood's movie. "Letters from Iwo Jima". If you were going to die anyway, why not fight to the end?

126

第3章　大東亜戦争

　一つの重要な理由は、ルーズベルト大統領による無条件降伏の要求でした。その宣言の意味は、日本国の存在、国民の命が奪われることを意味していました。もしかしたら、アメリカ人はただ単純に日本人を全員殺す、それとも奴隷にするかも知れません。アメリカ人は私にそのような話はナンセンスで、日本はそのまま降伏するべきだったと言います。しかし日本の立場から考えると、アメリカ人を信頼することは困難でした。戦争の前に、アメリカは常に外交で日本に損害を与えてきたからです。

　ジョン・ダワー氏の本『容赦なき戦争：太平洋戦争における人種&パワー』によると、アメリカ兵に降伏しようとした日本兵の半分は米兵からそのまま殺されました。クリント・イーストウッド氏の映画『硫黄島からの手紙』にもこのようなシーンが有りました。いずれにしても死ぬのなら、最後まで戦うでしょう。

The massive air raids designed to exterminate the Japanese civilian population did not inspire trust. When the Japanese leadership knew that America could not be stopped, the leadership searched for ways to force America to negotiate on terms that would at least preserve some part of Japanese being. What was most important was the preservation of the Imperial Household and the Emperor. This was the minimum goal of the Japanese leadership. Without the continued existence of the Emperor, Japan would have descended into chaos. And in the end, they succeeded.

　それと、日本の一般国民を絶滅させる為に考えられた大規模な米軍の空襲を考えると、アメリカ人を信用することは難しかったでしょう。アメリカの軍事的進行を止める事が不可能だと分かり、日本の指導者は出来るだけ国体維持の条件で、アメリカと交渉する方法を探りました。最も大切な事は、天皇陛下と皇室の維持でした。これは日本の指導者の最低限の目標でした。天皇陛下の存

在が続かないと、日本は混乱に陥るからです。最終的に、この目標は達成出来ました。

Also, battles like Okinawa were a delaying action. Japan had massed quite a lot of troops and Tokko aircraft in Kyushyu. It highly likely that the American invasion force would have been defeated. I think that Roosevelt's demand for unconditional surrender was a mistake. To Americans, it sounds very decisive. But Churchill himself was against it. He felt that Germany would have had an anti Hitler coup and surrendered earlier if Roosevelt had not insisted on it.

また、沖縄のような戦いは日本側の時間をかせぐ為の戦略でした。九州で日本軍が数多くの兵士と特攻隊の軍機を集めたら、アメリカの侵略部隊は負けたでしょう。 私はルーズベルト大統領の無条件降伏の要求は間違いだったと思います。アメリカ人にとってはそれはとても決定的なことのようです。イギリスのチャーチル首相は反対でした。彼は、もしドイツに対して無条件降伏の要求がなかったら、ドイツ軍がヒトラーを殺して政変した可能性が有ると考えていたからです。

Nanking Incident
南京事件

Let's talk about Nanking now. The story of Nanking is probably the center piece of Western anti Japanese propaganda. The image that Westerners, particularly Americans want to portray is that of cruel, nasty, and brutal mob. That is what they say the Imperial Japanese Army was. There are some Japanese scholars and commentators who say the story of Japanese brutality at Nanking was a lie.

Americans and other foreigners focus on these people to say that Japanese are unrepentant about the war. Why should Japanese be repentant? There is nothing to apologize for. America never apologizes for it's wars, and they did a lot worse things than Japanese troops ever did. And Chiang Kai Shek himself has admitted to exaggerating the figure of casualties at Nanking, in order to gain Western sympathy. Well, as I have written earlier in this book, he converted to Christianity to get help from America, certainly it could be assumed that he would use Nanking for propaganda purpose.

それでは、南京事件の話をしましょう。南京事件は西洋国の反日のプロパガンダの中心です。西洋人、特にアメリカ人が作りたいイメージは日本軍が残酷で、冷酷、とにかく悪の集団であるということです。世界に、日本帝国軍はそういう軍であったと見せたいのです。一部の日本の学者と評論家が南京事件の日本の残酷行為は嘘であると言っています。

アメリカ人や他の外国人はこの人達を見て、日本人は戦争について反省していないと騒ぎます。何故日本人は反省する必要が有るのですか？日本は謝罪する必要が有りません。アメリカは自分の戦争を謝罪しないですし、アメリカ兵は日本兵よりはるかに悪いことをしてきました。蔣介石氏は自分自身が、西洋国の同情を得る為に、南京事件の死亡者数を大げさに言ったと認めました。この本に書きましたが、彼はアメリカの援助を受ける為にキリスト教に改宗しました。やはり、南京事件をプロパガンダの為に利用しています。

But what is the truth? First of all, I think something did happen at Nanking. Were Chinese people killed and raped? Yes I think

Chapter 3 The Pacific War

so. Was the Imperial Japanese Army terrible? Well, it was a war. War is a very different environment.

I just cannot say that the Imperial Japanese Army was terrible. I was in the United States Marine Corps from 1974 to 1976. I was based in Iwakuni Japan. One day when dining off base, there was a Marine at the bar next to me. I did not know him. Suddenly, he started crying. I asked him what was the matter. He told me his story. He had been in Vietnam. One day on patrol, a child came to his best friend, some 10 meters away. The child held out a bundle of flowers. Inside the bundle was a bomb, both the child and his friend were killed. After that, every time a child came near him in Vietnam, he shot them dead. He was very afraid. Was he an evil man? No, he was not. Yet he killed many children. He cried when he remembered their ghosts.

　しかし真実は何でしょうか？　まず、南京で何かが有ったことは真実だと思っています。中国人は殺されたり、レイプされましたか？　私は有っただろうと思います。日本帝国陸軍は残酷でしたか？　その時は戦争でした。戦争は平時とは違う環境です。私は、日本帝国陸軍が残酷とは言えません。

　私は1974年から1976年米海兵隊として、山口県岩国基地にいました。ある日、基地の外のバーで飲んでいる時に、私の隣に座った海兵隊員がいました。私は彼を知りませんでした。突然、彼が泣き出したので、私が「どうしたの？」と尋ねると、彼は自分の話を始めました。彼はベトナム戦争で戦った兵隊でした。ある日、パトロール中に、子供が10メートル離れた彼の友達に花束をもって差し出しました。花束の中には、爆弾が入っていました。友達と子供が一緒に死にました。その事件の後、ベトナムで子供が近くに来るたびに、彼は射殺していました。とても怖かったのです。彼は残酷な男だと思いますか？　私はそう思いません。しかし、多くの子供を殺しました。その子供達を思い出し、罪の意識で涙

130

が出てしまうのです。

There is one great fact about Nanking that convinces me that there was no war crime committed there. In the Book "Soldiers of the Sun, the rise and fall of the Imperial Japanese Army" author Meiron Harries writes one extremely important point. At Nanking he mentions that there were only 17 Japanese military police to control 30,000 Japanese troops. They could not. After the battle, General Matsui increased the number of police, and an incident like Nanking never happened again.

Since there was no order to kill and rape, and since General Matsui took measures to control his troops, Nanking was a tragic event, but not a crime. In wars, people die. When battles happen in cities, civilians get caught up in it.The honor of the Imperial Japanese Army is intact, there is nothing to be ashamed of.

南京事件について一つの大きな事実が有り、これは戦争犯罪がなかったという証拠になります。この本、『Soldiers of the Sun: The rise and fall of the Imperial Japanese Army』の著者 Meiron Harries は大切なポイントを書いています。南京では、３万人の兵士を管理する為に 17 人の憲兵しかいなかったということです。この人数で兵士を管理することは不可能でした。南京戦の後、松井大将が憲兵の数を増やしたので、南京事件と言われるようなことは起こっていません。

市民を殺せとかレイプしろという命令はもちろん有りません。松井大将が兵隊達を管理、制御する為の措置を行なったのです。南京事件は悲劇的な事件だけれど、犯罪では有りませんでした。戦争では、人が死にます。大都市で戦いが有ると、一般市民が巻き込まれます。日本帝国陸軍の名誉は守られています。不名誉だと感じる必要は有りません。

Chapter 3 The Pacific War

America on the other, has never really tried to control troop behavior. In WWII, the only army that behaved worse than Americans was the Russians. American troops did many terrible things in the war, one was desecration of the dead.

They took Japanese body parts and used them as souvenirs. This was common in the Pacific war. US troops would even send these skulls home to their wives. President Roosevelt himself was presented with the forearm of a Japanese soldier as a letter opener.

それに比べて、アメリカは昔から兵隊の活動、態度を、あまり管理していません。第二次世界大戦で、アメリカ軍よりひどい態度の軍はロシア軍だけです。アメリカ兵は戦争で多くのひどい事をしました。一つは戦死した日本兵の体を冒涜したことでした。

戦死した日本兵の体の一部分をお土産として使用していました。大東亜戦争ではこういった事件がよく有りました。米兵は日本兵の頭蓋骨を自分の奥さんにお土産として郵便で送りました。

An American woman receives a Japanese skull from her boyfriend
アメリカ人女性は、戦場の恋人から日本人の頭蓋骨を贈られ受け取っていました
出典：『LIFE』1944年5月「Jap Skull」Wikipedia - http://en.wikipedia.org/wiki/American_mutilation_of_Japanese_war_dead

ルーズベルト大統領もこういったお土産、日本兵の前腕を使用して作られたレターオープナーを前線からお土産として貰いました。

This did not happen in Europe with the bodies of German troops. I have been able to find only one recorded incident in Europe where an American placed a German soldiers skull on a tank.

This is because Americans at the time did not regard Japanese as human. The practice was also common in the Vietnam war. American troops would cut off the ears of Vietnamese soldiers, and make necklaces out of them.

ヨーロッパではドイツ兵の死体に対してこのような問題はありませんでした。ヨーロッパの戦いで、一つだけ記録された事件しか見つけられませんでした。あるアメリカ兵がドイツ兵の頭蓋骨を戦車の上に付けたというものです。

何故こういう事が有ったかの理由は、当時のアメリカ人は日本人を人間と思っていなかったからです。この問題はベトナム戦争でも一般的でした。アメリカ兵はベトナム共産軍の耳を切り落として自分のネックレスを作りました。

And they do the same in Afghanistan today. When liberating France in WWII, American soldiers raped and stole their way across the country. For a full account, read "What soldiers do, sex and the American GI in World War II France" by Mary Louise Roberts.

In wars since then, like Korea, Vietnam, Iraq, and Afghanistan, American troops have behaved like baboons. A crime is planned away from the battlefield. By this definition, the holocaust that Nazi Germany did would certainly be a crime. I define a war

Chapter 3 The Pacific War

crime by this measure. What happens on the battlefield, under extreme stress, cannot be called a crime. Thusly, what happened at Nanking cannot be called a crime.

そして現在、アフガン戦争で同じ事を行なっています。第二次世界大戦でフランスを解放させた時、アメリカ兵はフランスのいたる所でレイプや強盗を働きました。細かい話は『What soldiers do, sex and the American GI in World War II France』(Mary Louise Roberts 著)を読むと分かります。

その後の戦争で、朝鮮戦争、ベトナム、イラク、アフガンで、アメリカ兵の態度は非常に凶暴でヒヒと同じです。犯罪とは戦場を離れて、計画をしたという事です。この意味で、ナチスドイツの大虐殺(ホロコースト)は勿論犯罪です。私はこの様に戦争犯罪を定義します。戦場での事件、とてもストレスが有る所で、その状況での事件は犯罪と言いません。南京事件もその一つに過ぎません。

The firebombing of Japan
日本の空襲

The same thing can be said about the American bombing of Japan. Japanese houses were built in America by the American Army. Fire bombs were then dropped on them, to learn how to burn them easily.

From the beginning, it was known by the American Army leadership that there was no need to bomb Japan. It was known that American submarines were destroying the Japanese merchant fleet. This prevented raw materials from reaching the factories on the Japanese main islands. Then the factories could not function.

So the goal of the American strategic bombing campaign from

the beginning was simply to kill Japanese people. And action like this was, at the time, recognized as a war crime. But no one in America thought to stop this. It is my estimate that at least some 2 million Japanese people, women and children, old people mostly, were killed.

　同じ事がアメリカによる日本空襲に言えるでしょう。アメリカ陸軍では、焼夷弾で効果的に日本式の木造の家を燃やす為に、実験用にアメリカ本土で日本式の木造の家を造りました。

　初めから、アメリカ陸軍のリーダー達は日本に空襲の必要がないと分かっていました。それはアメリカ海軍の潜水艦が、日本の貨物船を数多く沈没させていたからです。貨物船が沈没させられ、日本列島の工場に資源が届かなくなりました。その結果、日本の工場が機能しなくなっていました。

　ですから、初めから、アメリカの日本を空襲する目標はただ人

The firebombing of Tokyo
東京大空襲
出典：米軍撮影　パブリックドメイン

Chapter 3 The Pacific War

を殺すための事でした。当時でも、このような活動は戦争犯罪と認められていました。しかし、アメリカでは反対する人がいませんでした。私の見積もりでは２百万人、主に女性、子供、お年寄りが殺されたと思います。

In the March 10 1945 raid on Tokyo, the first bombers to arrive dropped their bombs to create a square of fire around Sumida ward. This was purposeful, to trap people in the target area. The following waves of bombers dropped their bombs in the center of the square. I think the casualty count of 100,000 for this raid of just one night is very low. It was mass murder.

1945年３月10日の東京大空襲の場合、最初の爆撃機は墨田区を囲う様に、四角く火の壁を作りました。これはわざと、墨田区の人々が逃げられない様にする為でした。その後に沢山の米軍の爆撃機がこの四角の中へ向けて焼夷弾を落としました。私は、この大空襲による一晩での犠牲者が10万人というのは、とても低い数字だと思います。この空襲は大虐殺でした。

There is something in the American soul that desires destruction. As America expanded across the Western plains, some 50 to 60 million Buffalo lived there. In the 1870's tours by rail were conducted. The sole purpose of these tours was to kill Buffalo. The trains would run until they came in the middle of a Buffalo herd. The train would then stop, and the passengers shoot Buffalo.

Now, the Buffalo is not an intelligent animal. Hearing a shot, and the Buffalo next to it falling down, will not alarm the herd. The only thing that would cause the Buffalo to run away would be the smell of blood. So by watching the wind, the train passengers could kill many Buffalo before they escaped. The corpses of the killed Buffalo were left to rot. In 1884, there were less than 2,000 left alive in America. This was an American pastime of that era.

　アメリカ人の心の中で、何か崩壊することを望んでいる事が有ります。アメリカは昔、大西部へ拡大を行なっていた時、そこには5千から6千万頭のバッファローがいました。1870年代に鉄道の観光が行なわれるようになりました。この観光の唯一の目的はバッファローを殺す為でした。その汽車はバッファローの群れを見つけるまで線路を走ります。群れを見つけると、群れの真ん中で汽車が止まり、乗客がバッファローを撃ち始めます。

　残念ながら、バッファローはあまり賢い動物ではありません。銃の音を聞いて、隣のバッファローが崩れ落ちても、別に何も危ないと感じません。危険を感じて逃げさせるものは、血の匂いだけでした。だから、風の方向を注意して撃ち殺せば、バッファローが逃げる前に乗客は数多くのバッファローを殺す事が出来ました。そこで殺されたバッファローの死骸は腐るまで放置されました。6000万頭いたバッファローも1884年にはアメリカ大陸に

Buffalo killing tourism in 1871
1871年、バッファロー殺しの観光
出典：Library of Congress

残された数は2千頭以下となっていました。これは当時のアメリカ人の娯楽でした。

Fear of the Christian Fundamentalists
キリスト教原理主義の恐怖

In more modern times, I found something much more scary. If you read my blog, you will notice that I write much about the present Christian Fundamentalist movement. At the present time, they are about 25% of Americans. The Christian Fundamentalists have concentrated particularly on conversions within the US military, and are strong in the Air Force and Army.

更に、現在のアメリカではるかに怖い話を見つけました。私のブログでは、現在のキリスト教原理主義について書いています。現時点でこの人達は、アメリカの人口の約25％です。キリスト教原理主義は、特に軍隊の中に集中していて、空軍と陸軍で改宗される傾向が強いです。

It has come to light a few years ago, that training manuals in the US Air Force for nuclear missile troops were filled with Bible quotes. The basic message of these quotes was to prove that Jesus loves nuclear war.

There are many of the Christian Fundamentalists who think thermonuclear war is desirable. Why? Well, since they believe correctly in Jesus, in their thinking, they are certain to go to heaven. So it would not matter if massive amounts of people, including themselves and their children die in a nuclear war.

数年前に、米空軍の核ミサイルを運用する兵士の訓練マニュア

第3章　大東亜戦争

ルには聖書のフレーズがたくさん引用されている事が明らかになりました。このフレーズの基本的なメッセージはイエス様が核戦争を愛している、それを証明することでした。

　キリスト教原理主義運動の中で、熱核戦争が魅力的であると熱心に考えている人がたくさんいます。何故？　まあ、彼らはイエス様を正しく信じていれば、必ず天国へ行けると信じています。それで、もしも自分と自分の子供も含めて、数多くの人々が核戦争で死ぬのであれば、それは構わないことだと考えています。

I grew up in the midwestern part of America. There, jokes about nuclear war were common. People would say it would be a good thing if New York, San Francisco, and Los Angeles were nuked by Russia because they were full of homosexuals, and America would be a better country with them all dead. Some people would even say the US Air Force should bomb those cities. I was horrified by such jokes, I just cannot find thermonuclear war to be a laughing matter.

　私はアメリカ中西部で育ちました。その地域では、核戦争のジョークをよく聞きました。例えば、もしソ連（当時）がニューヨーク、サンフランシスコ、ロサンジェルスに核兵器を落としたら、アメリカは助かります。どうしてですか？　その大都市はゲイの人が多いから、彼らが皆死んだらアメリカはもっと良い国になります。ある人の話では、アメリカ空軍がアメリカ西、東海岸の大都市に核兵器を落とすべきだと言いました。私は子供の頃にそのジョークを恐ろしいと感じました。やはり、核戦争は笑い事ではありません。

I will not only say Tokyo, or Hiroshima and Nagasaki, but the bombings of all Japanese cities were simply pure horror. When

Chapter 3 The Pacific War

I think of the same Americans today finding nuclear war an attractive option, I think that perhaps what America did to Japan was only the beginning of horror.

The American appetite for destruction, combined with the strict dogma of Christian Fundamentalism, produces a fearful combination. This is very frightening.

東京、広島、長崎だけではありません。日本の全ての都市への空襲は恐ろしいものでした。多くのアメリカ人が核戦争を魅力的だと思っていると考えると、もしかしたら、アメリカが行なった大東亜戦争の日本への空襲は、恐ろしい活動の始まりだったのかも知れません。

アメリカ人が持つ破壊欲求とキリスト原理主義が結びついた時、とても危険な終末思想が生み出されます。これは本当に恐ろしいことです。

Comfort Women (Camp Followers)
軍人相手の売春婦

What were the Comfort Women? As I write this book, South Korean government sponsored activists are actively engaged in undermining the reputation of Japan. They set up Comfort Women memorials in the United States and other countries. They are creating and exhibiting salacious comics of alleged Comfort Women experiences.

Well Comfort Women did indeed exist. It was a well run and administered system of prostitution by mostly Korean contractors for the Japanese military. It is a historical fact in all over the world that wherever armies move, women follow. There is such a word in English, "camp followers".

第3章　大東亜戦争

　いわゆる従軍慰安婦とは何でしたか？この本を書いている今、韓国政府が支持している活動家は、一生懸命日本の国際的な評判に傷をつけています。アメリカ合衆国やその他の国に従軍慰安婦記念碑を造っています。従軍慰安婦事件についてみだらな漫画を描いて、国際的イベントに展示もしています。

　慰安婦は居ました。しかしそれはほとんど朝鮮人業者が日本軍の為に経営した売春システムでした。歴史的な事実は、世界中で軍が移動すると女性があとに続いて付いて行きます。英語で〝camp followers〟という言葉があり、〝軍人相手の売春婦〟という意味です。

However, American and European countries never officially admitted this historical fact. Only the Japanese government officially admitted it and apologized for the prostitutes out of their own good will. That is why Japan is now accused by various parties.

In the American Civil war, General Hooker was a general of the northern Union Army, and the girls in the camps were called "Hooker's girls" after him. He was not a successful general against the southern armies, and was soon fired by President Lincoln.

　しかし、アメリカもヨーロッパの国も、決してこの事実を公式に認めません。日本だけが政府が公式に認めて謝罪しているために、世界から非難されているのです。

　売春婦について、もう一つの英語の俗語では〝Hooker〟と言います。この意味は女性がホックで男性を捕まえることではなく、アメリカの将軍の名前です。アメリカの南北戦争で、数多くの女性が軍に続いて付いて行きました。Hooker将軍は北部の連邦政府軍の将軍でしたので、その軍のキャンプにいた女性達はHookerの女性という名前が付けられました。　彼は南部の軍に対して戦

141

Chapter 3 The Pacific War

果を挙げることが出来ず、リンカーン大統領により解雇されました。

But such camp followers are a historical fact. They existed in any battlefield. Uncontrolled prostitution would mean an explosion of venereal disease in the army. Venereal disease has always been a serious problem for military units throughout history. Also, it was bad for discipline.

If you say the Comfort Women system is ultimately a matter of women's rights, you should investigate and compare the one of other countries in the war period. I am positive that Japan's system was the best in terms of hygiene and salaries for the women. It is unfair that only Japan is accused just because only Japan tells the truth.

　しかし、その〝軍人相手の売春婦〟は歴史的な事実です。どこの国の軍隊にもあったことです。売春は衛生面の管理をしていないと、その軍の中では性病が爆発的に増えました。人類の歴史の始まりから、性病は軍隊の大きな問題でした。それと軍の規律にも悪いことでした。

　慰安婦問題が女性の人権問題であると言うのなら、大東亜戦争中の全世界の慰安婦がどんな待遇だったのか調査し比較するべきでしょう。恐らく日本の慰安婦達が衛生面、待遇面で最も優遇されていたでしょう。日本だけが隠すことなくこの問題の調査に応じていて、そのために非難されているのは、アンフェアです。

To my knowledge, the Japanese Comfort Women system was the best run in the world. Other countries like France and America had such systems, but Japan's was the largest.

Yes, America had government sponsored prostitution centers

then. In Honolulu Hawaii. It was in a location called "Hotel Street". The whole point of this American Comfort Women system was to keep the Sailors and Marines from coming into the better parts of town, and harassing local girls for sex.

　私が知っている限り、日本の慰安婦システムは世界で最もよく管理されているものでした。別の国、例えばフランスとアメリカに慰安婦システムがありましたが、日本の方が大きくしっかりと管理されていました。
　そうです。当時アメリカ政府が管理している慰安婦センターがありました。場所はハワイのホノルルで〝ホテルストリート〟という所でした。このアメリカの慰安婦システムは、米海兵隊、水兵が街の良い所に来ない様に、良い家族の女性をナンパしない様に、という目的で始まりました。

And of course to prevent venereal disease. American Comfort Women did 100 men a day, each man had three minutes with a girl. He would wash his private parts with a disinfectant, the girl would also wash and come into his room. They would have sex, with condom, both wash afterwards, the girl would go on to the next room.

In recent years, Korean activists have started in America a campaign to discredit Japan. They are putting monuments to Korean Comfort Women. They are attempting to rename city streets, such as renaming Flushing Avenue in Queens New York "Comfort Women" avenue. They are contacting other ethnic groups to form a basis for cooperation against Japan.

　勿論、性病を防止するという理由も有りました。アメリカの慰安婦は一日100人の男と性交しました。各男性の時間は3分。兵士が下半身を洗って、慰安婦も体を洗い、部屋に入ります。コンドー

Chapter 3 The Pacific War

ムを付けてセックスをして、その後二人とももう一度体を洗って、慰安婦が次の部屋、次の男性の所へ行きました。

　最近、韓国人活動家達はアメリカ合衆国で日本の信用に傷を付ける為の活動をしています。従軍慰安婦記念碑を造り、道路の名前を変更しようとしています。例えばニューヨーク市、クィーンズ区でフラッシングアベニューを〝従軍慰安婦アベニュー〟という名前に変えようとしています。それから、日本を攻撃する為に、別のエスニックグループと協力的な組織を作る試みをしています。

I am particularly alarmed at Koreans working with Jewish groups. They are claiming the same victimhood status with Jewish people. They are saying that they went through the same holocaust.

Now I am a historian of WWII. For me, this is blasphemy of the highest order. I will say this categorically. The attempted extermination of Jewish people by nazi Germany in the second world war was a terrible, horrific event. I think that the magnitude of this event is still difficult for people today to understand. And that is why there are so many people today who are trying to deny that it happened. It becomes difficult for the average person to understand.

　私は特に、韓国人活動家がアメリカのユダヤ組織と組む事が危険であると思っています。韓国人は自分達がユダヤ人と同じ様な犠牲者だと言っています。韓国人の主張では、ユダヤ人と同じ様なホロコーストを日本から受けたと言っています。

　まず、私は第二次世界大戦の歴史研究家です。私にとって、この韓国人の活動は最大の冒涜です。はっきり書きます。第二次世界大戦のナチスドイツのユダヤ人絶滅の試みは恐ろしい、酷い事件でした。現在でも、この事件の巨大さは理解しにくいでしょう。

144

現在でも、この事件がなかったと言っている人がいます。普通の人は理解しにくい問題です。

It happened. But there is no way that Koreans can say that the Comfort Women system was the same type of terrible event for them. Today, foreign activists, primarily Koreans and American use the Kono statement as proof that the Japanese government did in fact coerce women into becoming Comfort Women.

However, the Kono statement was meant as a political gesture, and it's factual basis was extremely flawed. It was totally based on the testimony of 16 women only. Any responsible historian will tell you that for such a important judgement like this, you need more evidence than verbal testimony.

この事件は確かにありました。しかし、韓国人の言う、慰安婦システムとユダヤ人大虐殺事件が同等のことであったとの主張は

American military men line up for American Comfort Women in Hawai
アメリカ人慰安婦が働くハワイの慰安所に並ぶ米兵
出典：Axis History Forum「Hotel Street,Honolulu」

Chapter 3 The Pacific War

無理です。現在、外国の活動家、特に、アメリカ人と韓国人は河野談話を従軍慰安婦が強制的なものであった証拠として利用しています。

しかし、河野談話は政治的なものでした。根拠となる真実はありませんでした。この談話の根拠は、ただ16人の証言だけでした。どんな歴史評論家でも、こういう重要な判断の為には、ただの証言より証拠が必要であると言います。

There is no evidence. All stories that Japanese Army rampaged through villages dragging off women have been proven false. There was an extensive recruiting system, which was run by ethnic Koreans.The Japanese government in Korea did prosecute Koreans who cheated the girls. They were paid very good money, and lived good lives.

その証拠は有りません。日本帝国陸軍が当時朝鮮の村で暴れ回って強制的に女性を誘拐した、そのような話は全部嘘だという証拠があり、証明されています。当時、朝鮮人が経営した女性を公募する大規模なシステムが実際に有りました。当時、日本政府が朝鮮で女性を騙した朝鮮人を起訴しました。慰安婦の収入は良かったですし、良い生活が出来ました。

American feminists and Korean activists
アメリカのフェミニストと韓国活動家

Yet by starting this attack against Japan in America, they gained the support of the American feminist movement. American feminists have always disliked Japan. In my opinion, in American society, men are totally dominated by women. Women are demanding that society be rearranged to suit them.

A recent example of this is the recent changing of laws to allow women to serve in combat units, as regular combat soldiers. I am very glad to say that the United States Marine Corps has suspended this program. Physically, women just could not qualify. Well, 25% of the men who enter the US Marine infantry training do not qualify.

しかし韓国人活動家はアメリカでこの活動を始めて、アメリカのフェミニスト運動の支持を得ました。昔から、アメリカのフェミニストは日本が大嫌いです。私の意見では、アメリカの社会で、男は完全に女性に支配されています。アメリカ人女性の要求に合う様に、フェミニストが社会を作り直しています。

最近の実例は女性が軍隊の戦闘部隊に入る事が可能という法律に変わったことです。米海兵隊はこの提案を中止したという事で私は嬉しく思います。肉体的に、女性には無理です。まず、米海兵隊の歩兵訓練に参加する男性も25％が脱落します。

But this points out what American feminists want to do. They think that they can change reality to suit their own ideas of superiority. American feminists see Japan as a country where the women are totally dominated by men, and that Japanese women need to be saved by American women.

For them, Japan is an evil society. So when the Korean people in the US joined up with influential feminists, the result was that Japan was suddenly being labeled as a "Sex Slave" country.

しかし、このようなことから、アメリカのフェミニストが何を考えているのか見えてきます。フェミニスト達は、自分達の考える優位性に合わせ、現実を変える事が出来ると思っています。アメリカのフェミニストは日本では男性が女性を完全に支配してい

Chapter 3 The Pacific War

ると思っています。それと、日本の女性をアメリカのフェミニストが救う必要があると考えています。

　フェミニストにとっては、日本は最悪の国です。それで、韓国人活動家が影響力のあるアメリカのフェミニストと組むことになり、その結果、日本は突然〝性奴隷〟の国というイメージが付けられました。

I saw a lot of American feminists who came to Japan in the 1980's. They tried to create a feminist women's movement in Japan, but were spectacularly unsuccessful. Japanese women were just not interested in their message. They went back to America frustrated, and hating Japan.

Now, some of them are active in think tanks in the US, aiding Korean activists in any way they can to attack Japan. The Japanese government is not fighting back. But with Koreans starting to attack Japan in America, I am very happy to see that Japanese/Americans have woken up. And the way to fight back is with facts. Tell people in other countries that Koreans were indeed Japanese citizens at the time, not an occupied country.

　1980年代にアメリカのフェミニストが多数日本に来ました。日本で、フェミニスト運動をつくろうとしましたが、成功しませんでした。彼女達のメッセージに、日本の女性は興味がありませんでした。そのアメリカの女性は国へ帰り、心の中に失望、日本に対する嫌悪の気持ちを持つようになりました。

　現在、アメリカのフェミニストはアメリカのシンクタンクに働きかけ、日本を攻撃する為にどんな事でも韓国人活動家の支援をしています。日本政府は反撃をしていません。でも、韓国人は日本を攻撃する為に徐々にアメリカを利用しているので、反日的な日系人もいますが、多くのアメリカの日系人が目を覚ました事は嬉しいことです。反撃の仕方は、真実を使うことです。他国の人々

に、当時朝鮮人は本当に日本帝国の国民で、占拠されている国ではなかったという真実を伝えましょう。

The Contradiction of U.S. military
アメリカ軍の矛盾

The American military has not been able to solve their problem with rape. Today in the American military, one third of it's female members are raped, two thirds sexually assaulted according to "American Journal of Industrial Medicine" and other sources. During America's occupation of Iraq, rape happened everywhere. America started the Iraq war with 53 cruise missile strikes, designed to kill the top 53 leaders of the country. There was no declaration of war.

All those strikes did not hit the intended target. When America conquered Baghdad, those leaders hid. So American troops arrested their wives and children. In prison, the women were raped. I saw pictures of this on the internet.

現在、アメリカ軍はレイプの問題の解決を出来ません。

「American Journal of Industrial Medicine」他によると、現在のアメリカ軍で、3分の1の女性兵はレイプされて、3分の2は性的暴行を受けています。また、アメリカのイラク占拠時に、イラクの至る所でアメリカ兵によるレイプが起きました。アメリカはイラクの指導者達を殺す為に、53発の巡航ミサイルによる攻撃でイラク戦争を開始しました。この時宣戦布告は全くありませんでした。

その巡航ミサイルによる攻撃はどれも、目標のイラク指導者には当たりませんでした。アメリカがバグダッドを占領した時に、その指導者達は隠れてしまいました。その為、アメリカ兵がその

Chapter 3 The Pacific War

指導者達の奥さんと子供を逮捕しました。拘置所では、女性がレイプされました。私はインターネットでその写真を見た事があります。

America and Great Britain executed 1,100 Japanese Imperial troops after the war for water boarding. Yet lawyer John Yoo for the Bush administration, declared it legal for Americans to do the same torture in Iraq. He said that when Americans do it, is more humane. I don't think so. In all wars, terrible things happen. The Japanese military tried to instill more discipline in it's troops to correct these problems when it happened. While America has always tried to hide it's problems, and cover them up.

America, China, and South Korea are always making accusations against Japan. Now I will give an example of how to fight back against such accusations. First of all, Americans think of such a conversation as a battle. One person will win, one person will lose. Japanese think of such conversations as a way to create mutual understanding.

大東亜戦争後、アメリカとイギリスは日本帝国軍人1,100人をウォーターボーディング（水責めの拷問）の罪によって死刑としました。しかし最近、ブッシュ政権の弁護士ジョン・チュン・ユ氏が、イラクでアメリカ兵が同じ拷問を行なう事は法的に正当であると宣言しました。彼は、アメリカ人が拷問を行なう場合は、人道的であるという意見です。私はそう思いません。どんな戦争でも、ひどい事件が起きます。何か問題が有った時に、日本帝国軍はより強い規律を作り、守らせるようにしていました。一方のアメリカはいつも問題を隠しています。

アメリカ、中国、韓国の3ヵ国は、常に日本に対する非難をしています。これから、その非難に対する反撃の方法を教えます。まず、アメリカ人は会話は戦いであると考えます。誰かが勝ち、

誰かが負ける。日本人にはお互いに理解しあうという考えが有ります。

Everybody knows how Comfort Women memorials are being put up in the US. In particular the statue at Glendale California. I have heard that a member of Nippon Ishin no Kai went to Glendale to protest, and met with a Glendale city council member. When the Japanese politician announced his intention, the American said. "Do you know about Nanking?"

The Japanese politician became flustered, and not knowing how to answer, the meeting was over. Well, in America, Americans will intentionally say such provocative things. When Japanese have a discussion, everybody tries to find a point of cooperation. When Americans have a discussion, they try to destroy the other person's point of view, and force their own ideas on other people.

　最近、アメリカ国内で従軍慰安婦の記念碑が作られています。カリフォルニア州グレンデール市では慰安婦像が作られました。日本維新の会のメンバーが抗議の為にグレンデール市へ行ったという事を聞きました。グレンデール市議会の議員と会って、それで自分の訪問の理由をアメリカ人に伝えると、そのアメリカ人の返事は「南京について知っていますか？」

　この返事に、その日本の政治家はあわてふためいて、どう返事をしたら良いかが分からなくて、ミーティングが終わりました。まあ、アメリカではアメリカ人が意図的にこのような挑発的な事を言います。日本人は議論をする時に、皆の妥協点を探します。アメリカ人は議論をする時に、他の人の立場を潰すようにして、自分の考えを他の人に強要します。

Chapter 3 The Pacific War

An example of a debate
ディベートレクチャー

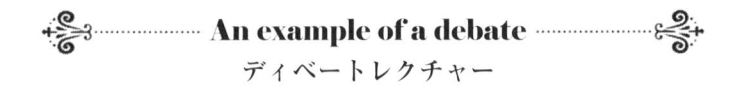

So how should the Japanese politician have spoken? I will give an example.

それでは、日本の政治家はどうしたら良いでしょうか？　以下の私の例を参考にしてください。

Japanese politician: I am here to protest the Comfort Women Memorial statue in Glendale. It can only harm American/Japanese relations.

日本人政治家：私はグレンデール市の従軍慰安婦記念碑に抗議する為に来ました。この記念碑は日米関係を悪化させるだけのものです。

American official: Do you know about Nanking?

アメリカ人議員：南京について知っていますか？

Japanese politician: Do you know about My Lai? Such events as that happened a thousand times over in Vietnam.

So you know about Abu Ghraib? Such abuses were system wide in the prison system in Iraq. Most Iraqi's detained by the American forces in Iraq were innocent of any attack on America.

日本人政治家：ソンミ村虐殺事件を知っていますか？　ベトナム戦争でそのような事件は何千回もありました。

アブグレイブ刑務所における捕虜虐待を知っていますか？　その虐待はイラクの刑務所ではどこでもありました。アメリカ軍が逮捕したイラク人のほとんどはアメリカに対して悪い事をしてい

152

ません、無実でした。

Do you know about Guantanamo? Most of the detainees there have committed no crime. Yet they remain in detention.

At Nanking, General Matsui increased the number of military police in further operations. At the battle of Hankow, such events did not reoccur. So it can be said that the Japanese Imperial Army could restore discipline itself.

　グアンタナモを知っていますか？ほとんどの抑留者は犯罪を犯していません。しかし、彼らはそのままキューバのアメリカ軍収容所に収監されたままです。
　南京では、その戦いの後で松井大将が憲兵の数を増やしました。その結果、漢口の戦いでは問題が発生しませんでした。そのことからも、日本帝国陸軍は自分達で規律を強化し、守れたという事がわかります。

Rape is something that the American military has not been able to control for years. Even today one third of US female military members are raped. But Mr. American official, Nanking and My Lai and Abu Ghraib have nothing to do with our discussion today. Today we are speaking about the Comfort Women statue. Korean people are lying and exaggerating about the Comfort Women issue.

It was a well managed system, the girls were safe and well paid. Today, Korea is jealous about Japan, because it was Japan that bequeathed modern civilization to Korea. They could not do it themselves. By erecting this Comfort Women statue, you are participating in this dispute between Japan and Korea. Don't you think that this is an international policy matter, and outside the realm of the City of Glendale to deal with?

Chapter 3 The Pacific War

　レイプは何年もの間アメリカ軍がコントロールすることが出来ていません。現在でもアメリカ軍の女性兵士の３分の１はレイプされています。
　当時の日本軍相手の慰安婦は衛生面をよく管理されていましたし、女性の方は良い収入を得ていました。現在、韓国が日本に対して抱くコンプレックスは、日本が現代的な文明を韓国にもたらしたことです。当時の朝鮮人は、自分達では近代化することは出来ませんでした。この従軍慰安婦記念碑を建てたことで、貴方は日韓問題に入りこんでいます。しかし、これは国際的な問題でしょう？この問題に入りこむ事はグレンデール市の領域ですか？

American official: ?????????

　アメリカ人議員：？？？？？

　My Lai was a massacre of unarmed women and children in a Vietnamese village in the Vietnam war. The officer in charge was tried and found guilty. But all throughout the Vietnam war, such incidents happened.
　Abu Ghraib was the torture and abuse of Iraqi detainees during the Iraq war. Most of them had committed no crime, but simply got caught up in American sweeps of local areas.
　The abuses at Abu Ghraib received a lot of attention, a few low ranking soldiers went to prison. But there were wide spread reports in the media and net that the abuses were rampant in all American administered detention centers in Iraq.
　Some Japanese people might feel that such a conversation is way too confrontational, that it is rude. Well, that is how Americans

talk. If you do not show strength, they will think you are weak, and you have lost the conversation.

　ソンミ村虐殺事件はベトナム戦争の戦地の村に住んでいる武器を持っていない女性と子供の大虐殺事件でした。指揮をとっていたアメリカ士官は裁判にかけられ、有罪になりました。でも、ベトナム戦争ではそのような事件は数多く起こりました。

　アブグレイブ刑務所ではイラク戦争の抑留者に対する拷問や虐待がありました。イラク抑留者のほとんどは犯罪を犯していない、アメリカ軍が街や村を巡察している時に逮捕された人達です。

　アブグレイブ刑務所における捕虜虐待はよくマスコミに報道され、数人のアメリカの下級兵士が有罪となり、刑務所に入りました。しかし、アメリカのマスコミで、このような拷問は全てのイラク内のアメリカ軍が支配する刑務所で行なわれていたという報道が有りました。

　日本でこういう議論は、対決的で失礼と考える人が多いでしょう。でも、アメリカ人はこのように議論します。議論では強い立場で話さないと、あなたが弱い立場であると考えられ、負けです。

　Americans think of such conversations as a battle, in all affairs, trade, government negotiation, even marriage.

　Yes, in marriage, legal contracts are common in American society. They are called pre nuptial agreements. If you break the contract, you can be legally punished by a court, or divorce may result. This is how Americans think, as Japanese, we must deal with Americans as they are.

　Yes, it is very possible that the American official would explode in anger in this conversation. However, frankly speaking, in such a case, the conversation is completely lost from the beginning, there is really no point in continuing.

　If the Japanese politician tried to find a common point in such a

Chapter 3 The Pacific War

case, he would be wasting his time. Instead of searching for an area to cooperate, he should have prepared a list of nasty things done by the US and South Korean militaries. He should have had more information.

アメリカ人はどんな事でも議論は戦いだと思っています。貿易、政府と政府の交渉、結婚でも、全ては戦いだと考えています。

そうです。アメリカ社会の結婚では法的な契約書を交わすことがよく有ります。婚前契約と呼ばれています。もしその契約書の条件を守らないと、裁判で罰せられるか、離婚の原因となります。

アメリカ人はこの様に考えます。日本人はそういうアメリカ人に対応しなければなりません。

まあ、前述の会談で、アメリカ人議員は怒る可能性が高いです。しかし、正直に言うと、その場合、初めから会談が無駄ですし、議論を続けても意味が有りません。

このような場合に、もし日本人政治家が妥協点を探すとしたら、時間の無駄です。妥協点を見つけるのではなく、アメリカ軍、韓国軍、世界の酷い事実をひたすら列挙していくのです。その為にもこちらは沢山のカードを持っておくべきです。

The Tokubetsukogekitai
特別攻撃隊

Tokubetsukogekitai, or in English, is the Special Attack Corps, is the proper name for the units that were called "Kamikaze" by Westerners. There were aircraft operated by both the Imperial Army and Navy, purpose built torpedoes piloted by a human, and explosive filled motor boats, both of these last operated by the Navy. The Imperial Navy also planned on using divers carrying explosive charges to sink landing craft during the invasion of mainland Japan.

Americans are terrified of the concept of the Tokkotai. They simply cannot comprehend it. For Americans, at least most of them, they cannot understand the concept of willingly sacrificing one's own life.

An American might sacrifice themselves to save their own child in a dire situation, but it would be impossible for them to do so for something as abstract as the nation. They would surrender first.

　西洋人が〝神風〟と呼ぶ部隊の正式な名前は特別攻撃隊です。この部隊の武器は帝国陸海軍の軍機、海軍の人間が操縦する魚雷、それと爆発物を積んでいるモーターボートでした。帝国海軍は他にも、アメリカ軍が日本列島に上陸する時に海岸で爆弾を持ったダイバーを使って上陸艇を破壊する計画がありました。

　アメリカ人は特別攻撃隊の概念をとても恐れています。まず理解出来ません。ほとんどのアメリカ人は、自分の人生を犠牲にす

Special Attack Corps members
特別攻撃隊
出典:「毎日グラフ」1965 年 11 月 25 日臨時増刊号　パブリックドメイン

Chapter 3 The Pacific War

るという概念を理解することは出来ません。
　まあ、非常事態の時に、自分の子供の命を救う為に、自分の命を犠牲にするということはあるかも知れませんが、国の為にはしないでしょう。その前に降伏します。

For the American, much more than the nation, their own life is important. Recently, we have seen an example of this. In 2003, American President Bush invaded Iraq and Afghanistan. While many Americans publicly cheered these wars as revenge for the 9/11 disaster, the number of volunteers for the military was very small. Americans declined to disturb their daily lives, take the risk of death for the American Middle Eastern wars. And the American government did not dare try to instate a military draft, there would have been social revolt.

American society just does not have the inclusiveness of Imperial Japan, or even of Japan today. A person is not simply just an individual life, he is part of a family, part of a nation.

In these modern times, the ties to nation are not as strong as they were in Imperial Japan. However, the bonds of family are much stronger than in America. Also, there is a concept of belonging to the group that is all Japanese, that is much stronger than what feelings Americans may have for their country.

　アメリカ人にとっては、自分の人生が全てです。最近の実例があります。2003年に、ブッシュ大統領がアフガンとイラクに侵攻しました。多くのアメリカ人は9・11のテロの復讐としてこの戦争を公然と歓呼し応援しましたが、軍隊の志願者の数は非常に少数でした。大多数のアメリカ人は自分の毎日の生活を捨ててまで、死ぬ可能性が有る中東戦争へは行きませんでした。当時アメリカ政府は、反乱、革命を恐れて、軍隊を徴兵にすることは出来ませ

んでした。
　アメリカの社会は、大日本帝国、或いは現在の日本の様に包括的では有りません。日本では、人はただ個人ではなく、家族の一人、国の一人という絆があります。
　現在の日本では、国民と国の絆は大日本帝国時代のようには強く有りません。しかし、家族の絆はアメリカよりとても強いです。それと、すべての日本人は日本人グループに属する一人という概念と気持ちは、アメリカ人が国に対して持っている気持ちより強いです。

I do not think that Americans understand the concept of their own country. They talk of such ideas such as freedom, but they do not possess and spirit of sacrifice to defend the nation.

Instead, they interpret freedom to mean the right to gratification, self satisfaction. This is achieved by the accumulation of things, material goods. There is little room left over in the hearts of modern Americans to think of sacrifice for the nation.

Post war, Japan has been affected by this disease. When I first came to Japan 40 years ago, many Japanese could only think of buying designer goods, or trips overseas. Yet I am very pleased that the younger generation today does not care so much for material things, but seems to place more importance on being Japanese.

　私は、アメリカ人は自分の国の概念を理解していないと思います。自由についてはよく話をしますが、国を守る為に犠牲となる気持ちは持っていません。
　逆に、自由の意味を自分が満足する権利だと思っています。この満足は物質、財産を蓄積することでなし遂げられます。現在のアメリカ人の心の中に、国の為に犠牲となることを考える場所は有りません。

Chapter 3 The Pacific War

　戦後、日本もこの病気の影響を受けています。40年前に、私が初めて日本へ来た時に、数多くの日本人はブランド品を買ったり、海外旅行のことしか考えていませんでした。しかし現在の日本の若者を見ると、とても嬉しいです。物質、財産では無く、日本人がどういう存在であるかを考える事を大切にしているでしょう。

Americans in general demonize any Japanese attempt to praise the sacrifice of the Special Attack Corps. They are very critical of such movies as "The Eternal Zero", or the movie "Yamato". Americans prefer movies by left wing directors that portray the Special Attack Corps as victims of duplicitous Japanese leaders. They try to downplay their courage and sacrifice.

Could I do the same thing? I am a former military man, but would I willingly go on a one way mission for my country? Well, I am 58 years old as I write this, it is not likely that will again see active military service. But I think that such a question like that can only be answered on the battlefield itself.

As for the members of the Special Attack Corps, they have my tremendous respect. As a historical note, there is one other country that I know that used such Special Attack units in combat. That is Germany.

　基本的にアメリカ人は、日本人が特別攻撃隊を称賛する試みをディモナイゼーション（悪魔化）しています。『永遠の0』とか『男たちの大和』といった映画に特に批判的です。
　アメリカ人は日本の左派の監督が作っている映画、特別攻撃隊の兵士達が、日本の指導者に騙された被害者だったという映画を好みます。アメリカ人は特別攻撃隊の勇気、犠牲を軽視しています。
　私は同じ事を出来るでしょうか？　私は元軍人ですけど、祖国の為に片道の使命、帰れる望みのない役目をまっとう出来るでしょうか？まあ、私はこの文章を書いている現在58歳です。もう一

度現役軍人にはならないでしょう。しかし、そのような質問の返事は戦場でしか出来ないでしょう。

　特別攻撃隊の兵士の方々を、私はとても尊敬しています。

　歴史的にみると、もう一つ戦場で特別攻撃隊を使った国がありました。それはドイツでした。

The German Air Force was desperate to stop Allied air attacks on German cities. Towards the end of the war, It was decided to send young pilots on one way missions. At that time, an American fighter pilot had some 365 hours of flight training before going into combat. A new, young German pilot would have only 11 hours. There was no hope of their survival or being able to shoot down Allied aircraft in normal combat. So it was decided to have the young pilots ram Allied bombers, and take them down on a one to one basis. These tactics were employed on two occasions. Unlike Japanese Special Attack units, half of the young German pilots actually survived ramming a bomber, and were able to parachute back to the ground.

　ドイツ空軍は、ドイツの大都市への連合国軍の空襲を止める為に必死でした。そして戦争の末期に、若いパイロットを特攻：片道の使命に使う事が決められました。当時、戦場へ行く前に、アメリカ人パイロットは365時間、訓練の時間がありました。ドイツの若く新しいパイロットは、戦場へ行く前にたった11時間しか訓練の時間がありませんでした。普通の戦闘では、このドイツの若いパイロットが連合国軍の軍機を撃ち落とし、生き残るという望みはありませんでした。それで、この若いパイロットが連合国軍の爆撃機に激突して、1対1で落とす作戦が決定されました。

　この作戦は2回使われました。日本の特別攻撃隊と違って、ドイツの若いパイロットの半分がこの作戦で生き残ったのは、激突の前に陸まで落下傘で降りたからでした。

Chapter 3 The Pacific War

Today, in Japan, it is easy to find commentary that in the war Japan was hopeless in all respects, and was led into the war by evil Japanese leaders. This is complete American propaganda. One thing they keep saying is that Japanese military equipment was inferior to America, so war was hopeless.

Not at all. I will now go into a little detail about the Imperial Japanese Navy. Japanese Heavy Cruisers and destroyers were the best in the world in The Pacific war. The Myoko class, the Takao class and the Mogami class, with ten 8 inch guns and their torpedo reloads made them the most formidable heavy cruisers in the world at that time.

The newer Japanese destroyers at the start of the war carried six guns and torpedo reloads. American destroyers did not carry reloads, so once they shot off their torpedoes, that was that. The torpedo was the weapon with which a destroyer could sink a much heavier ship.

And Japanese torpedoes were the longest range and best in the world at the time. For the first year and half of the war, American torpedoes malfunctioned and did not explode half of the time.

　現在の日本では、大東亜戦争は完全に絶望的で、当時の日本の指導者が悪かったというコメントを見つけることはとても簡単です。これは完全にアメリカのプロパガンダです。一つのプロパガンダは日本の装備はアメリカの装備と比較すると粗悪だったというものでした。だからアメリカに対しての戦争は絶望的だということです。

　全然違います。日本帝国海軍に対して細かく書きます。日本の海軍重巡洋艦と駆逐艦は、大東亜戦争当時、世界で最強でした。妙高型重巡洋艦、高雄型重巡洋艦、最上型重巡洋艦は、10門の20cm大砲、予備の魚雷があり、当時の世界で一番強い重巡洋艦

第3章　大東亜戦争

でした。

　大東亜戦争開始当時に、日本の駆逐艦には大砲6門と予備の魚雷が有りました。アメリカの駆逐艦には予備の魚雷がなく、魚雷を撃ったら、攻撃は終わりでした。魚雷は駆逐艦が、駆逐艦よりもはるかに大きい軍艦を沈没させる事を可能にする武器でした。当時、日本の魚雷の射程距離は世界で最も長距離でした。大東亜戦争の最初の1年半で、アメリカの魚雷はよく機能不全があり、半分位爆発しませんでした。

In carrier operations, at the beginning of the war, Japan was superior to America. For example, consider the two cruisers Tone and Chikuma. These were heavy cruisers, carrying eight 8 inch guns, but the gun turrets were all placed on the forward section of the ship.

The after section had six reconnaissance float planes. These planes provided the "eyes" of the carrier fleets, searching out

Myoko class heavy cruiser
妙高型重巡洋艦
出典：Japanese Navy　パブリックドメイン

Chapter 3 The Pacific War

enemy ships. For reconnaissance, Americans used bombers from their carriers. This procedure took strike aircraft away from attack duties, and also had to be flown and recovered from the carrier deck. This meant that such time for flying reconnaissance missions interfered with strike missions.

The Japanese procedure of using dedicated ships with float planes for reconnaissance was superior.

航空母艦の作戦では大東亜戦争の初期、日本はアメリカより優勢でした。例えば、重巡洋艦利根と筑摩を考えましょう。20cmの大砲8門があり、砲塔は全て軍艦の前方に配置してありました。

その重巡洋艦の後半分にある甲板の上には6機の偵察機がありました。この偵察機は機動部隊の〝目〟として敵の軍艦を探していました。偵察の為に、アメリカは航空母艦に搭載されている爆撃機を使いました。これにより爆撃機の任務が攻撃では無く偵察となり、その為に航空母艦から離艦、着艦する時間が、他の攻撃に向かう戦闘機、爆撃機の任務遂行を邪魔していました。

日本の、着水偵察機を重巡洋艦に搭載して偵察を行なう、というやり方は優れていました。

Most American leaders had a poor opinion of the Japanese Imperial Navy before the war. Secretary of the Navy Frank Knox felt that America would win a war with Japan in six months. Officers of the American Asiatic fleet in the Philippines had observed the Imperial Japanese Navy, they knew that Japanese ships were powerful and well handled. Their comments were ignored in Washington.

The only reason Japan lost the war is because America could replace lost ships, Japan could not because of lack of resources.

The Agano class light cruiser, the Matsu class destroyer, these ships were small. The Agano had only six 6 inch guns, compared to 15 for an American Brooklyn class. The Matsu was really the size of a corvette.

Late in the war, Japan just could not produce aircraft carrier engines. So the Unryu class of carriers were powered by destroyer engines set up in tandem.

　戦前は、ほとんどのアメリカの指導者達は日本帝国海軍を下に見ていました。フランク・ノックス海軍長官は、アメリカと日本が戦争となったら半年で勝てると考えていました。フィリピンに居たアメリカのアジア艦隊の士官達は、日本帝国海軍の作戦を観察していたので、彼らは日本の軍艦は強く乗組員が優れていると知っていました。彼らの報告はワシントンでは無視されていました。

　それでは、何故日本が負けたのか。それは、アメリカは軍艦を失っても新しく軍艦を作り、戦場に投入することが出来ましたが、日本にはそれが資源不足で不可能だったことです。

　阿賀野型軽巡洋艦、松型駆逐艦、この軍艦は小さかった。阿賀野は大砲6門しかなかったのに対し、アメリカの軽巡洋艦ブルックリン型は大砲15門がありました。松型は本当にコルベット艦の大きさでした。

　戦争の末期には、日本は航空母艦のエンジンを製造する事が不可能でした。なので、雲龍型航空母艦の葛城は駆逐艦エンジンを縦に並べて搭載されました。

All through the war, the Imperial Japanese Navy showed a remarkable ability to innovate with what they had. The conversion of the battleships Hyuga and Ise, and the heavy cruiser Mogami had their after turrets removed to build an aircraft flight deck for seaplanes was unique. The Hyuga and Ise were designed to handle 22 planes, and the Mogami 11 aircraft.

And of course, The Battleships Yamato and Musashi were the

Chapter 3 The Pacific War

biggest and most powerful battleships in the war. The 3rd ship in the class, the Shinano, was converted into an aircraft carrier. She was the biggest in the world at that time, in my opinion she could have operated 120 aircraft.

As for the Imperial Japanese Army, American writers often say that Japanese leaders were stupid, ordering Banzai charges on American forces. And that Japanese soldiers were also stupid robots.

　大東亜戦争中、日本帝国海軍は自分達の持っている物で驚くべきものを開発する能力がありました。戦艦日向と伊勢、それと重巡洋艦最上に施された、軍艦の後ろ部分の砲塔を除去して、着水軍機の甲板を作るという改造はとてもユニークでした。日向と伊勢は22機、最上は11機の航空機を保有出来る様に設計されました。

　勿論、戦艦大和と武蔵は、当時、世界で最も大きく、強力な戦艦でした。3番目の戦艦、信濃は、航空母艦に転換されました。

Battleship carrier hybrid Hyuga
航空戦艦日向
出典：Japanese Naval Warship Photo Album: Battleships and Battle Cruisers
パブリックドメイン

私の意見では120機の軍機を載せる事が可能でしたので、当時の世界最大の航空母艦でした。

　日本帝国陸軍の場合、アメリカの評論家はよく日本の指導者は、アメリカの部隊に〝万歳攻撃〟を命令した愚か者であったと言い、日本兵は愚かなロボットであったと言います。

What Americans mean by a "Banzai charge" is a form of assault by the Imperial Japanese Army. Troops would simply charge an enemy position, screaming "Banzai". The position would be taken in bayonet fighting. Before meeting up with the Americans, the experience that the Imperial Japanese Army had was in China. Chinese forces in general were weak. They had large numbers of troops, but few supporting arms, like machine guns and mortars. They were usually not paid, and poorly fed. A strong infantry assault by the bayonet was usually enough to send them running. Americans however, had many machine guns, mortars, also Naval artillery, and air superiority. Charging into such a position would result in the destruction of the attacking force, with no effect upon the Americans. So as the war went on, Japanese troops learned to dig in. And fight to the last man. The battles of Iwo Jima, Okinawa, and Peleliu were very costly and shocking for America.

　この〝万歳攻撃〟とは、帝国陸軍の強襲の一形態でした。兵士は「万歳」を叫びながら、敵陣を銃剣で戦い、占領します。アメリカ軍と戦う前にあった日本帝国陸軍の戦争の経験は、中国との戦いでした。中国軍の部隊は弱かった。兵士の数は多かったのですが、支援火器、例えば機関銃、迫撃砲は少なかったですし、兵士は給料をほとんど貰えず、食料も十分には貰えていませんでした。日本軍の強力な銃剣による攻撃で、大抵は中国軍が走って逃げました。

　しかし、アメリカ兵は機関銃や迫撃砲の数は多く、さらに軍艦

Chapter 3 The Pacific War

の大砲、航空戦の優位もありました。そのような強い敵に攻め入っても、攻撃部隊は絶滅に到り、アメリカの部隊には影響ありませんでした。それで、徐々に日本兵は穴を掘ることで対応し、最後の一人まで、絶滅するまで戦いました。硫黄島、沖縄とペリリューの戦いで戦死したアメリカ兵の数の多さは、アメリカ人にとってはとても衝撃的でした。

Whenever I hear Americans say that Japanese soldiers were robots, I know I am speaking with a fool. There is something in American society that admires defiance of authority. Why? The only reason I can see is to show off one's ego. Many Americans take pride is saying that they know more than the boss. Or by demanding that everything be explained to them in detail before a job is begun, and that their cooperation be requested by management.

When I worked in the film business in Tokyo, I often had this problem with Americans. I was a location manager for an office supplying foreign extras, for Japanese film and television productions.

アメリカ人と会話すると、そのアメリカ人は、日本兵はロボットだったという話が始まり、その度に、愚かなアメリカ人と会話をしていると感じます。アメリカ社会では、官憲に反抗的な態度をとる事が魅力的だという感覚があります。何故？　私はこの気持ちをよく理解出来ませんが、多分自分の自我を誇示するためでしょう。仕事場で、多くのアメリカ人が社長や上司より知識が有る事を同僚に言い、その話を誇りに思っています。また、どんな仕事でも始める前に、経営者に細かく説明させて、自分に仕事への協力をお願いすることを望みます。単に、自分が偉いと思っているのです。

　昔、私が東京のフィルム業界で働いていた時、アメリカ人とこ

168

のような問題がよくありました。私は、日本の映画、テレビ番組の制作に外国人エキストラを提供する、数千人が登録している外タレ事務所の現場マネージャーでした。

Everyday, I would be at some location easy for foreigners to find, such as Shibuya Hachiko, or Shinjuku station west exit police box, at 6:30 in the morning. I would meet up with foreigners, take them to the studio or location bus. I would then be the manager and translator for the shoot that day.

I knew a bad day was coming when things like this would happen. I would meet 10 or 15 people, checking their names off a list. I would then introduce myself to everyone, telling them I was their manger for the day.

Someone, always an American, would say, "Nobody told me you are the manager, I am not listening to you." What this person means is, he is such a great and fantastic person, he will not obey anyone, everybody has to see to his satisfaction. Needless to say, it is nearly impossible to work with such a person.

　毎日、私は朝6：30位に外国人が簡単に見つけられる場所、例えば渋谷ハチ公、あるいは新宿駅西口交番等で色々な外国人と待ち合わせをして、撮影現場、それかロケバスへ連れて行きます。その一日、私はマネジャーと通訳の仕事をします。

　このような事があると、その日は一日大変だという事が分かります。例えば、10人から15人位が集合するのを待ちます。待ち合わせ場所に人が来ると、リストで名前をチェックします。皆が集まったら、自己紹介をして、そこに集まった外人達に、私がその日のマネジャーである事を説明します。

　いつも、アメリカ人の誰かが、「貴方がマネジャーという事を聞いていない！貴方には従いません！」と言います。この人の言いたいことは、自分は素晴らしい人間だから、誰にも従わない、

169

Chapter 3 The Pacific War

皆が自分の欲求を満足させなければならない、ということです。勿論、そのような人とは仕事になりません。

One particularly difficult day, was with the American Air Force. The day before the location shoot, we called the families with specific instructions. We were using American children, and the rule was one parent or guardian per child. There were a lot of people involved, the location busses would be very crowded, so the day before we made sure that the families understood that no extra people could come. I was the manager on that job. There were 5 American children involved. That means we had allotted ten seats on the bus for them.

They brought their entire families. Mother, father, sisters and brothers, even school friends. Why? They all wanted to watch their little child be a TV star. When I reminded them that they had been told only one parent could accompany the child, they told me that without their children, we could not make the film.

　アメリカ空軍の軍人の子供を使った日は大変な一日でした。撮影の前の日、撮影をする具体的な内容を説明するため、その家族に電話をしました。内容は、アメリカの子供を使う再現ドラマでした。子供一人につき、親も一人という決まりでした。何故か。この仕事は多くのスタッフが必要だったので、ロケバスはとても混みます。そのため、前日に皆に連絡をして、余分な人が来ることは出来ないと説明しました。私はその日のマネージャーでした。子供5人を使うので、ロケバスで割り当てられた席は10席です。

　この子供5人は家族全員で集合場所まで来ました。両親、兄弟、学校の友達まで来ました。何故？皆はその子供の撮影しているところを見てみたいと思っていたからです。それで、私がこのグループに子供一人親一人のルールのことを言うと、ある親が「私たちの子供がいないと、貴方は仕事が出来ません！」と言いました。

170

第3章　大東亜戦争

They demanded that we get some extra buses. Just especially for them. Well the leader of this nasty American Air Force group was a Sergeant. I am a former Marine myself, I knew how to talk to them. My reply was "Hey! I am a regular drinking buddy of your base Colonel, your commanding officer. I think in our next beer session, I will bring up your name, and what you people did here today!"

The truth was, I did not even know the name of the base colonel. Of course, I never went beer drinking with him. But it scared the Americans enough, that the extra people went home.

彼らは、「私達に別のバスを用意しなさい！」と要求してきました。彼達の欲求を満たす為に。このグループのリーダーは空軍の軍曹でした。私は元海兵隊ですから、軍人とどう話したら良いか、よく分かります。私はこう対応しました、「おい！私は貴方の基地の大佐とよくビールを飲む友達だ。次に飲む時に、貴方の名前と今日貴方のした行動を話すことになるだろう！」

本当は、その基地の大佐の名前も知りませんでした。勿論、一緒にビールを飲んだ事はありませんでした。でも、その話を聞くと、余計についてきたアメリカ人達は恐がり、家に帰りました。

This is why Americans make such poor soldiers. A military organization cannot function if a leader has to always ask for the cooperation of his men. In a military organization, it functions well when soldiers immediately respond to orders.

Also, in recent wars, American soldiers in general do not function well without massive firepower in support. In the book, "This Kind of War" about the Korean war, the author describes the ordeal of the American 2nd infantry division in Korea.

Chapter 3 The Pacific War

When North Korean and Chinese troops counter attacked, the division attempted to retreat to the rear. They ran into an ambush and disintegrated. Officers attempted to give orders to attack.

But the men ignored them, insulted them, and preferred to remain under the cover of their vehicles. They preferred to wait and be taken prisoner. In that war, they were lucky if the Chinese captured them. If the North Koreans captured them, they would be killed on the spot.

アメリカ人はそのままでは良い兵士にはなりません。もし軍の部隊長が常に部下にお願いしなければ動かないのであれば、組織は機能しません。兵士達が即座に命令に従うのであれば、軍組織が上手く機能出来ます。

最近の戦争では、大規模な火力の援護がないと、アメリカ兵はあまりよく戦いません。朝鮮戦争の本『This kind of war』の著者は米第2歩兵師団の苦しい体験を説明しています。

北朝鮮軍と中国軍が反撃をした時に、攻撃を受けた師団が後方へ撤退しようとしましたが、敵の待ち伏せに遭い、この師団は崩壊しました。待ち伏せに対して、その時士官達は攻撃の命令を出しました。

しかし、兵士達は士官を無視して、トラックの下に隠れる等して、捕虜になるまで待っていました。この戦争で、もし中国軍の捕虜になっていたら、それは運が良かった。何故なら、北朝鮮軍の捕虜になったら、その場で殺されたからです。

By my studies, it is the American Marines and US Army Airborne who are tough fighters. I myself am a former US Marine. A lot of our basic training was designed to get rid of such individualistic thinking, and produce men who can fight as a team.

And very aggressively. I finished basic training just at the end of the Vietnam war. My training sergeant, in his farewell speech to

第３章　大東亜戦争

our platoon talked a little bit about Vietnam.

He said that in the Vietnam war, new Marines, 30% could expect to be dead in the first year. That is because the Marines fought aggressively, and sent in infantry units in close combat to get the enemy. Just like the Imperial Japanese Army.

However, egotistical Americans, they call us Marines robots, people who cannot think individually.

　私の研究では、アメリカの海兵隊と陸軍空挺兵はチームとして強力に戦います。私は元海兵隊です。海兵隊の基礎訓練は個人的な考え方を無くす為のものです。チームで戦う為の兵士を作る訓練です。

　とても攻撃的に兵士を訓練します。私はベトナム戦争の最後の時に基礎訓練を終わりました。訓練軍曹が、小隊へのお別れのスピーチで、ベトナムの戦争について話しました。

　彼は、ベトナム戦争で、最初の一年にこの新しい海兵隊の３割が死ぬでしょう、と言いました。海兵隊は攻撃的に、敵軍と接近して戦うからです。帝国陸軍と同じ様です。

　しかし、自己中心的なアメリカ人は、海兵隊の兵隊は個人的に考える事が出来ない、ロボットと呼んでいます。

I look at such people, and smile. One, because I know that they are worthless, and two, because I know that I am stronger than them.

　私はそのような話を聞くと、その人を見て、微笑みます。その人は価値がない人で、私はその人より強いということが分かるからです。

Chapter 3 The Pacific War

Japan, the first nation that declared racial equality
人種の平等を最初に謳った日本

　There is one important aspect of the war in the Pacific that still terrifies Americans today. Japan long strived for racial equality with Western powers. They refused to consider it, Japanese people were still treated as second class.

　In the Pacific war, Japan had two basic goals. One was to ensure access to resources so that Japan could survive as a modern state. The other was to remove Western colonial power from Asia.

　The fall of Singapore, the Philippines, and defeat of Western Naval forces had a great impact of the thinking of Asian people. It showed that White people could be defeated by Asians.

　現在でも、アメリカ人が恐がっている、大東亜戦争のもう一つの重要な側面があります。明治維新から、日本は長い間に西洋国との人種平等、人種差別のない社会を作る為の努力をしました。西洋の国はそれを考える事も拒否し、その国々の国民にとって、日本人は２級国民でした。

　大東亜戦争の日本の基本的な目標は二つでした。一つは資源へのアクセスを確実にして、近代国家としての存在を守る事。もう一つは西洋の植民地宗主国をアジアから追い出すという事でした。

　シンガポールとフィリピンの陥落、西洋海軍艦隊の敗戦は、アジアの革命活動家の考えに大きな影響を与えました。これで、アジア人が白人に勝つ事が出来るのだと。

　Japan understood that Japan and other Asian countries could never be free as long as they were dominated by Westerners.

174

第 3 章　大東亜戦争

　The Co-Prosperity Sphere was announced in 1940. It envisioned an Asia led by Japan, which would bring prosperity to it's members, free of colonialism.

　Many nationalist movements sprang up in support of this. In India there was the Azad Hind and the Indian Independence League. In Indonesia, the Indonesian Nationalist Party, and in Malaysia Kesatuan Melayu Muda. Cambodia had the Khmer Issarak and in Burma there was Dobama Asiayone.

　日本の当時の指導者達の理解は、西洋人の国がアジアを支配する限り、日本とアジアが自由になることは不可能だということでした。

Japanese General Doihara inspects Indian National Army soldiers
日本帝国陸軍大将土肥原賢二がインド国民軍兵を閲兵中です
出典：World War II Database　　http://ww2db.com/image.php?image_id=11055

175

Chapter 3 The Pacific War

　1940年に宣言された大東亜共栄圏は、日本がリーダーとなっているアジアという哲学が有りました。アジアから西洋国の植民地をなくすことが目標でした。

　この運動を支持している愛国的なグループが沢山出来ました。インドでは自由インド仮政府、Indian Independence League、インドネシアではIndonesian Nationalist Party、マレーシアではKesatuan Melayu Muda、カンボジアには、Khmer Issarak、ビルマ（現ミャンマー）にはDobama Asiayoneがありました。

　Armed forces allied with Japan included some 40,000 Indian National Army troops, 11,000 Burma National Army troops, and there was PETA in Indonesia, which had 37,000 troops in Java and 20,000 in Sumatra.

　After the end of the war, these Japanese sponsored independence armies had a great effect in Asia. The British Raj in India tried to try in court some 5,000 members of the Indian National Army as traitors. They were formally of the British Army. At the fall of Singapore, they joined the Indian National Army and allied with Japan.

　日本と同盟していた軍隊はインド国民軍の4万人、ビルマ国民軍の1万1千人、インドネシアのPETAはジャワに3万7千人、スマトラに2万人の兵士がいました。

　戦後、これらの日本がスポンサーとなった独立した軍隊が、アジアに大きな影響を与えました。戦後のインド英国植民地政府が、インド国民軍の5千人を裏切り者として審理しようとしました。彼らは元英国軍兵でした。シンガポール陥落後、インド国民軍に入軍して、日本と同盟を結びました。

　However riots ensued across the country. Indian sailors in

176

第3章　大東亜戦争

the British fleet mutinied. People in the West think that it was Mahatma Ghandi alone who threw out the British Empire. Not at all. When these riots happened, Great Britain knew that they would badly lose a fight to keep India. So they decided to give up their Empire.

The PETA forces formed a backbone to the independence movement in Indonesia. A four year war was fought as the Dutch tried to keep their Empire. But in the end, it was impossible. And in Indonesia, thousands of Imperial Japanese Army troops joined the struggle.

　しかし、この裁判が始まるとインド全国で暴動が起こりました。英国海軍のインド人水兵も反乱を起こしました。西洋人達は、マハトマ・ガンディー氏が一人で大英帝国を追い出したと考えました。そんな事は有りません。そのような暴動が起こり、英国はインドを植民地として維持する戦いは勝ち目がないという事を理解しました。それで、インド植民地を放棄するという決断をしました。
　戦後、インドネシアでオランダが自らの帝国を維持するための戦争をしました。その戦いではPETAの兵隊は独立軍の中心として戦いました。4年間戦って、結果、オランダが負けました。そのインドネシアでは、何千人もの日本帝国陸軍の兵士がインドネシアに残って、独立軍と一緒に戦ったのです。

This is a very important aspect of the Pacific war, White people cannot understand it, so they try to explain the Special Attack Corps by calling them " emotionless robots". However, I have a question for Americans. Don't you think there is something much deeper involved here?

　大東亜戦争の重要な側面である、白人と有色人種の戦いを理解できないのであれば、特別攻撃隊も感情ないロボットとしてしか

177

Chapter 3　The Pacific War

理解できないでしょう。しかし、私は本当にそれだけなのか、とアメリカ人に問います。そこにはもっと何かあるのではないかという思いを私は持っています。

第 4 章　戦後

Chapter 4　After the War

Chapter 4 After the War

After the war, both Japan and America found common ground in the Cold War.

Frankly speaking, once the Japanese ground forces were recreated post war, an invasion by the Soviet Union became impossible. However, a submarine blockade of Japan could have been done by the Soviet Union.

戦後、日本とアメリカの両国は冷戦で共通の敵が見つかりました。

率直に言って、日本が戦後陸上自衛隊を作ってから、ソ連の侵略は不可能になりました。しかし、ソ連はまだ潜水艦で日本の海底封鎖をすることが可能でした。

Masochistic Japanese
マゾヒスティック（自虐的）日本人

When I first came to Japan, 1974, it was 29 years since the end of The Pacific War. So basically, men who were 50 years or older were veterans of the Imperial Armed Forces. I found them to be people of confidence. Having been in the military, and having fought, that gave them that confidence. There were however, the people who had just missed being in the military.

At the time I first came to Japan, they were in their 40's and 30's. As I write these lines in 2014, they are now in their 70's or so. They are the generation that is controlling Japan. When I first came to Japan, people of this age worshipped America. Everything about America, to them, America was a land of the Gods.

People would pay you a lot of money just to speak in English. It was easy to find a girl to have sex with if you were an American.

But for me, this was very embarrassing. When I grew up in America, it was in rural Wisconsin. People in general were not very educated, there was no job opportunity. It was a depressing place.

　私は1974年に日本に来ました、大東亜戦争の終戦から29年後でした。それで、基本的に50歳以上の男の人は帝国陸海軍の経験者で、自信がある人達でした。軍隊と戦場での経験がその自信を与えていました。しかし、ぎりぎり軍隊に入らなかった人も居ました。
　私が初めて日本に来た時の、その帝国軍の経験が無い人とは30代と40代でした。現在、日本の指導者達の世代です。その頃、この世代はアメリカを崇拝していました。彼らには、アメリカは神の国でした。
　彼らはただ英会話をする為に、たくさんのお金を払いました。アメリカ人でしたら、セックスをする女性を簡単に見つける事が出来ました。しかし私の場合、この様な事に違和感を感じました。私の出身はアメリカ、ウィスコンシン州の田舎でした。その辺りに住んでいる人たちはあまり教育が無くて、良い仕事のチャンスはありませんでした。住んでいて憂鬱な所でした。

When I came to Japan, it was like a wonderland. It was clean, people very polite and hardworking. I first came to Iwakuni in Yamaguchi Prefecture. I knew of course that this was the Japanese countryside. But even there, people were very educated. People actually knew more about American history than I did.

But why this worship of America? I think it was the post war era, the "Give me Chocolate" era. These people had grown up in a Japan that was extremely poor after the war. Yes, It was true that a Japanese girl post war would have sex with an American soldier for a chocolate bar.

Chapter 4 After the War

　そんな私が初めて日本に来た時、まるで不思議の国でした。そこは清潔でしたし、人々は丁寧で、一生懸命働いていました。私は最初山口県岩国市に来ましたが、そこは日本の都会ではなく、地方だという事は知っていました。しかし、地方でも、住んでいる人々の教育レベルは高いものでした。私よりアメリカの歴史の知識がありました。
　どうして日本人がこんなにアメリカを崇拝したのでしょうか？
　やはり戦後の〝ギブミーチョコレート〟時代は一つの原因でしょう。終戦直後に育った日本人はとても貧しかった。チョコレートの為にアメリカ兵とセックスをする女性も居ました。

Even after the immediate post war period, people would watch American movies and imagine that was how all Americans lived. Well, movies are a fantasy, when I grew up in America, I certainly

Japanese children receiving chocolate from Americans
日本の子供達は進駐軍放出のチョコレートを貰っています
出典：毎日新聞社（1946年）

did not live that way.

Most Japanese people simply worshipped America when I first came. I tried to tell people that really, for most Americans, life was not that fantastic. In fact, I told people in Japan, if I were to compare quality of life, Japanese people were much better off.

　戦後の時代が終わっても、日本人はアメリカの映画を見て、それが普通のアメリカ人の生活だと考えています。まあ、映画は空想の世界ですが、私はアメリカで映画の様な生活ではありませんでした。
　私が初めて日本に来た時に、数多くの日本人がアメリカを崇拝していました。私は自分の周りの日本人に、ほとんどのアメリカ人の生活はそんなに立派ではないという真実を伝えました。当時の生活の質を比較すると、日本人の生活の方がアメリカ人より全然良いと言いました。

Japanese people refused to believe me. Really, I did not have many girlfriends. Girls would date me, but always the question about getting married and moving to America came up, that was the end.

I loved Japan. When I told them about my studies of Japanese military history, and how I went to Yasukuni shrine, they thought I was crazy.

　日本人は私の言うことを信じませんでした。お蔭で、あまりガールフレンドが出来ませんでした。デートをしても、いつもその女性から「結婚して、アメリカで生活をする」という話が始まり、その関係が終わりました。
　私は日本を愛していました。そのデートをしている女性に、私の日本帝国陸海軍の勉強、それから靖国神社を参拝する事を教えると、その女性は私の事を頭がおかしい人だと思いました。

Chapter 4 After the War

Today, there is a lot of friction between Japan and America. The generation that presently leads Japan still holds those ideas about America being a perfect wonderland. And if you combine this with American ideas of being perfect, of American exceptionalism, we have a very dangerous combination.

現在、日米関係でトラブルが多いです。現在の日本を率いる世代は今でもアメリカが完全に上位の国だと思っていることが原因です。その考えと、アメリカ人が持つ、自分が例外の国であるという考えが交わると、危険な状態になります。

Americans always boast. But in, let us say trade negotiations, the present Japanese generation of leaders automatically believe what Americans say even if there are some conflicts. They do not examine the conditions of the agreement to see if it benefits Japan. They assume America is benevolent "Big Brother." America is not at all benevolent. Americans enter into negotiations with an eye to achieve American profit. Japanese profit or benefit is irrelevant. Well pretty any much any country does this. That is what negotiations are for.

And these masochistic Japanese also assume a stance that Japan is wrong, uncivilized, compared to America. That is why I call them masochists. I really think this kind of foolish personality is unique to Japan.

アメリカ人はいつも自慢をし過ぎています。でも、例えば貿易交渉で、現在の日本の指導者達は多少の衝突はしても自動的にアメリカ人の言うことを信じます。指導者達は日本の利益になるかどうかを、その交渉の細かい条件を見ません。アメリカは優しい〝兄〟と仮定しています。しかし、アメリカは全然優しくありませ

ん。アメリカ人が交渉をする目的は、自分の利益を取る為で、日本の利益は関係有りません。まあ、どんな国でも交渉ではそのように進めます。交渉とはそういうものですから。

　自虐的な日本人は、いつもアメリカと比較すると、日本が悪く、自国は未開の国という立場を前提とします。それで、私は自虐的と呼びます。やはり、このような愚かな人がいるのは世界で日本だけではないでしょうか。

There are several English language newspapers in Japan. One I have read The Japan TImes for nearly 40 years. They seem to search for things bad about Japan. If they cannot find anything, they take an event and write about it with a very anti Japanese stance.

For example, the paper I have noticed for 40 years, publishes a column by a certain person. This person has changed from American to Japanese nationality. But his reason for the change was not because he loves Japan. He decided to change Japan from the inside, to something more like America. For example, he would like to make Japanese human rights laws to be the same as American laws. Here, he is behaving like a typical American. And he provokes or fakes many of the events he uses in his articles.

　日本ではいくつかの英字新聞が有ります。その中の一つのジャパン・タイムズを私は40年間読んでいます。この新聞は日本の悪い事を探している様に見えます。何かを見つけることが出来ない場合は、その時にあることをとても反日の立場で書きます。

　その新聞である人の論文を載せています。その人はアメリカ国籍から日本国籍に帰化しました。しかし、この人の帰化の理由は、日本を愛しているという事では無いです。日本を中から変えたいという気持ちがあり、もっとアメリカの様な国に変えたいと考え

Chapter 4 After the War

ています。例えば、日本の人権法をアメリカの法律と同じ様にしたいでしょう。やはり典型的なアメリカ人の態度をとっています。そして、自分の記事で書く事件はほとんど自ら捏造しています。

He became famous for a lawsuit over an onsen in Otaru Hokkaido, which barred foreigners. Well, there are many Russian fisherman in the area, sometimes they get drunk. And barring foreigners is to prevent trouble. Yes, to say foreigners cannot enter is indeed wrong. But this person uses very confrontational tactics.

Years ago, in the G-8 conference in Hokkaido, he waited at the baggage claim in the airport. He stood there for along time. Finally, when a policeman came over and asked for his ID, he screamed "Prejudice! I am Japanese!". In such an environment of an international conference, it is natural that security people would question a person who seemed suspicious. He had his tape recorder ready to record the incident. He fakes his stories, just like the supporters of the Comfort Women.

その人は、北海道小樽市の温泉について訴訟を起こした事で有名になりました。この温泉に、外国人は出入り禁止でした。小樽市では酔っぱらいのロシア人漁師が問題を起こしていたので、その対策でした。もちろん外国人を温泉に出入り禁止にする事は間違っています。しかし、この人はとても敵対的な作戦を使っています。

数年前の北海道のG-8会議で、彼は千歳空港の手荷物受取所で待っていました。長い間そこで立っていました。そのうち、日本の警察官が身分証明書を見せて下さいと尋ねると、この人は「差別している！私は日本人だ！」と叫びました。国際会議が行なわれる環境で、怪しい人に警察官が話しかける事は当たり前です。この人は自分で仕込んだ事件を録音する為にテープレコーダーを

準備していました。〝従軍慰安婦〟支持者と同じ様に、この人は自分の話を偽造しています。

No person in the Western world would publish such garbage. Yet some people at this English language newspaper think this person, who attacks Japan, is significant. Such Japanese people think that foreigners are always right. They see Japanese culture as inferior to the West, particularly America. They believe that anything in America should be done in Japan. And they end up destroying many unique aspects of Japanese culture.

This is extreme masochism. This ridiculous concept is unique to Japanese people.

　西洋では、どんな出版社もこのゴミの様な記事を載せません。でも、この英字新聞では誰かがこの人の日本に対する攻撃的な記事が大切であると思っているのです。このような日本人は外国人が常に正しいと思っています。彼らは、西洋、特にアメリカの文化と比較すると、日本文化の方が劣っていると考えています。この人達は、アメリカで行なわれている事は、全て日本で行なった方が良いと信じています。それで、日本文化の素晴らしいものを潰そうとしています。

　これは超マゾヒスティック（自虐的）な行動です。世界で日本人だけの愚かな思考です。

For example, I have heard that in Japanese schools, the "every one is a winner", type of philosophy is being used in school games. This idea comes from American feminists who believe the cause of the world's problems is men. If competition between men could be eliminated, every where there would be peace. Unfortunately, it produces men who cannot function. America is a

Chapter 4 After the War

society teetering on collapse. Should we in Japan imitate that?

　例えば、日本の学校で、「1人1人が勝者です」という哲学が学校のゲームで利用されています。この哲学はアメリカのフェミニストが始まりです。彼女らは、世界の問題の原因は男であると考えています。もし男同士の競争が無くなれば、世界が平和になると。残念ながら、この哲学は機能不全な男を作り出しています。アメリカの社会はまもなく崩壊です。日本はそれを真似するべきだと思いますか？

And that is part of the problem with Comfort Women trouble, or what Japan did in the war. The Kono Statement is one example of such masochism. And it hurts Japan badly. I think it was done quickly in the hope to help the Japan-Korea friendship. And it was written to please Koreans, truth was not considered or sought.

　そして、それ（自虐的精神）は、慰安婦問題、或いは日本が戦争で行なった事の問題の一つです。河野談話はそのような自虐的なことの例で、日本はそのお蔭で厳しい損害を被っています。それは日韓の友好を願って急いで作られました。そして、韓国人を喜ばせる為に作られ、その真実は関係ありませんでした。

Many Japanese people easily assume that their family members are in some kind of trouble. That they may have done something wrong. In America, people would never, ever assume their own family member is wrong. Often, people in Japan apologize to smooth over social difficulties. The Japanese language is very self depreciating, one always places the other party above them. This type of thing is very important in Japan, but does not at all work well with foreigners.

188

第 4 章　戦後

　多くの日本人は問題が起きた時に、まず自分の家族が悪かったのではないかと考えます。アメリカでは、アメリカ人は絶対に自分の家族が悪かったのではないかとは考えません。日本では謝罪は社交辞令の為にも使います。日本語を使うと、自分の方が下の立場、相手の方が上になります。日本では、この様な事がとても大切ですが、外国人との付き合いでは混乱が生じます。

　America is a very legalistic society. So they will look at the Kono statement, and assume the worst about Japan, because it is a voluntary apology.
　Such masochistic Japanese, by always treating foreigners like Gods, are a barrier between the reality of Japan and the rest of the world. It makes it more difficult for foreigners to understand true Japanese thinking. Foreign government officials and businessmen just don't have time to meet people outside their line of work. Therefore, they can't understand Japanese. Very unfortunately, Americans have always favored such masochistic, America worshipping Japanese as leaders. They simply are afraid to trust normal Japanese people.

　アメリカは法律的な社会です。そして、アメリカ人が河野談話を見たら、自発的な謝罪ですから日本は最悪であると考えます。
　このような自虐的日本人が、外国人を神様のような扱いをすると、日本と他の世界との間に壁を作ります。このお蔭で、外国人が日本人の本当の考えを理解しにくくなるのです。外交官と外資系ビジネスマンは、自分の仕事以外の人とは交流する時間が無いので日本人を理解出来ないのです。残念ながら、昔から、アメリカ人は自虐的な日本人、アメリカを崇拝する日本人を指導者として支持しています。普通の日本人を信用する事を恐れています。

Chapter 4 After the War

It is in people under the age of 60 that I place my hopes for the future of Japan. And Americans, you need not fear them.

私が考えるのは、60歳以下の日本人は日本の将来の為の望みです。そしてアメリカ人へ、彼らを恐れる必要はありません。

About Yasukuni Shrine
靖国神社について

I would like to write about Yasukuni shrine. With the Yasukuni shrine, the issue of 14 Class A war criminals is not the only issue. Americans deeply fear Japanese history and culture, thus they push Chidorigafuchi National Cemetery as an alternative.

次に、靖国神社について述べます。アメリカ人にとって靖国神社の問題は、A級戦犯14人だけではなく、日本の歴史と文化を恐れていることにあります。だから、国立千鳥ヶ淵戦没者墓苑をその代替に推しているのです。

America is a new country. Americans are always suspicious of history. In America, historians are not respected. Americans live totally in the present.

When I first came to Japan in 1974 to Iwakuni in Yamaguchi prefecture, I visited nearby Itsukushima shrine. I was entranced by it. In particular, I was fascinated by the history. The present shrine was established in 1168. Other Americans were not very impressed by it. Oh, they would say it was beautiful, but if one started to compare the history of Japan with America, they quickly would get uncomfortable, then angry.

Americans always have to emphasize the superiority of America.

Yasukuni shrine
靖国神社

I think this is a reason why Americans are so destructive when they wage war. They simply do not like other countries' history, they want to erase it. At the time Itsukushima shrine was established, Europeans did not even know of the existence of the American continent.

　アメリカは新しい国です。アメリカ人は常に歴史のある国は危険であると思っています。アメリカでは、歴史評論家は尊敬されていません。アメリカ人は現在ある事しか考えないからです。

　1974年、私が初めて山口県岩国市に来た時に、近くの厳島神社へ行きました。そしてその神社にはうっとりしました。特に、その神社の歴史に魅了されました。現在の厳島神社は1168年に造られたものです。他のアメリカ人はあまり感銘を受けていませんでした。まあ、「美しいですね」とは言いますが、日本の歴史とアメリカの歴史と比較すると、すぐ気まずくなり、彼らは怒り出し

Chapter 4 After the War

ます。
　普通の会話でも、アメリカ人は常にアメリカの優位性を強調することが必要です。やはりこれがアメリカ人が戦争でとても破壊的である理由だと思います。彼らはただ単に、他国の歴史が嫌いですし、それを消したいという気持ちがあります。厳島神社が造られた時に、ヨーロッパ人はアメリカ大陸の存在さえ知りませんでした。

The Tokyo War Crime trials was conducted very hurriedly. The truth is, the laws that Japanese leaders were tried and executed for were basically just made up on the spot and it was against the basic concept of law, in any culture. In times past, when a country won a total war against another country, often the losing king or leader was simply killed.

But America wanted to make a legal show of winning the Pacific war. Racism was definitely involved. Japan as a non White non Christian country, being able to challenge White Christian America, was terrifying for the American elite. So the trials were extremely flawed. Once they began, there was very little doubt as to what the verdict would be.

　東京裁判はとても急いで行なわれました。その真実は、日本の指導者を裁判にかけ、処刑した法律が、その場の都合に合わせて急ごしらえで作られた法の概念に反するものだったということです。昔の戦争では、ある国が勝った時に、負けた国の王または指導者が殺されました。
　しかしアメリカは、大東亜戦争に勝ったことを示す法的なショーを作りたかったのです。間違いなく人種差別が関係していました。日本は白人でも、キリスト教でもない国なのに、アメリカに挑戦することが出来るということで、アメリカのエリートにとって恐ろしい国でした。東京裁判は非常に欠陥が多い裁判でし

た。これは始めから、判決は決まっていました。

Americans become very angry whenever any Japanese Prime Minister, or politician visits Yasukuni Shrine. They see this as a revival of Japan being a military nation. Yet America pushes Japan to participate in collective defense with America. So why get angry about Yasukuni shrine?

They fear that if Japanese leaders worship at Yauskuni shrine, it is Japanese culture, not controlled by Americans. That is why American leaders push Chidorigafuchi as an alternative. If leaders were to worship there, Americans would be reassured that they are under American control. Because of his visit to Yasukuni shrine, and his conservative views, Americans are very concerned that Prime Minister Abe will start another war.

　日本の総理大臣、政治家などが靖国神社を参拝するとアメリカ人が怒ります。日本が再び軍国主義になると思っています。しかし、アメリカは日本にアメリカとの集団的自衛に参加するように圧力をかけています。それなのに何故、靖国神社の事に怒るのでしょうか？
　アメリカ人の恐れは、日本のリーダーが靖国神社に参拝する場合、それはアメリカ人がコントロール出来ない日本の文化であるということです。アメリカ人が支配出来ていないという不安を持つのです。それで代替案として千鳥ケ淵戦没者墓苑を勧めています。もしそこへ日本の指導者がお参りすると、アメリカ人が日本の指導者をコントロール出来ているという事で安心します。安倍総理大臣の靖国神社の参拝と保守的な考え方によって、アメリカ人は安倍総理大臣がもう一度戦争を始めるのではないかと深く心配しているのです。

Chapter 4 After the War

 This is an American obsession, which I call "Looking for Hitler". The idea is that if British Prime Minister Chamberlin had been more strict with Adolf Hitler at the 1938 Munich Conference, WWII would not have happened. Well, that is a simplification. But since Americans always doubt and fear world leaders, they are searching for signs that some leader is going to go crazy and start a war.

 アメリカ人の妄想が有ります。私は〝ヒットラー探し〟と呼んでいます。これは1938年のミュンヘン会談で英国のチェンバレン首相がドイツのヒットラーに厳しかったら、第二次世界大戦は起きなかったというものです。まあ、それは複雑な話を単純化しているのですが、アメリカ人はいつも世界の指導者を恐れ、疑いを持っています。いつもアメリカ人はどこかの国の指導者がおかしくなり、戦争を起こしそうだという兆しを探し警戒しています。

 The American idea is that America should start a war first and win over evil, and save the world. In 2003, just before the Iraq war, Saddam Hussein was portrayed as the next Hitler in the American media.

 I wish to reassure my American readers; Prime Minister Abe is not Hitler, Japan is not going to start a war. Japanese are simply having pride in their country, that is all. Actually, the souls interred at Yasukuni shrine did nothing wrong. People accuse Tojo Hideki of being a criminal for starting aggressive war. What about George Bush invading Iraq for no reason? There is no difference.

 アメリカ人の考え方は、その悪の指導者が戦争を始める前に、アメリカが先に戦争を始めて、その悪い国、指導者を倒して、世界を救うべきだというものです。2003年に、イラク戦争直前、サ

ダム・フセイン氏はアメリカのマスコミによって次のヒットラーであるかのように描写されました。

　私のアメリカ人の読者の方、安心して下さい。安倍総理大臣はヒットラーではありません。日本は戦争を始めません。日本人はただ自分の国に誇りを持っているだけです。それが全てです。実際、靖国神社で祀られている人たちは悪い事をしていませんでした。アメリカ人は東條英機氏を侵略戦争を行なった犯人だと告発しています。でも、アメリカのブッシュ大統領が意味もなくイラク戦争を開始した事はどうですか？　何も変わりません。

I visit Yasukuni shrine twice a year to pay my respects, on August 15th, and December 8th.

　私は一年に2回、靖国神社に参拝に行きます。8月15日と12月8日です。

A letter to America
アメリカへの手紙

I would think that by now, if my American readers are still here, they are not very happy. I have not simply repeated American myths of moral superiority. Well, actually, I am accusing Americans of being nothing more than human. You see, American exceptionalism is the myth. And as a former Marine, I risked my life for you.

So yes, I think I have a right to comment.

　まあ、ここまで読んできたアメリカ人の読者は、あんまり嬉しくないでしょう。私はアメリカ優位の神話を書いていません。実際、私はアメリカ人は〝普通の人間〟であると言っているのです。

Chapter 4 After the War

やはり、アメリカは例外だという話は神話です。私は元米海兵隊で、その当時アメリカの為に命をかけました。
　そう、だから私はコメントする資格があります。

　As I write this, in 2014, it seems that so many Americans are still fighting the Pacific War in their hearts. Why? Japan did lose the war, that is not disputed.

　For it's part, Japan has done it's best to be a good friend and partner of the United States. But I think too many Americans assume the worst about Japan. And that is too bad. Japan is the one country in Asia that used to genuinely like Americans.

　Oh! I say used to. Well the Japanese opinion of America is shifting, and not in a good direction. I think I could say, Japanese are disappointed in America.

　2014年に私はこの本を書いていますが、数多くのアメリカ人は心の中では、まだ大東亜戦争を戦っている様です。日本が負けたのに何故？
　日本は、一生懸命にアメリカの友好国として、良いパートナーになる努力をしました。にも拘わらず、日本が悪いと簡単に仮定するアメリカ人が多過ぎます。とても残念です。最近まで、日本人は本当にアメリカ人が好きでした。
　否！私は最近までと述べましたが、正直に言うと、日本人のアメリカ人に対する意見がだんだんと変わってきています。日本人はアメリカに対して落胆しています。

　In this book we have seen how Japanese people had an intense curiosity about Americans when the Black Ships first came at the end of Edo era.
　Before the war, American culture, jazz, novels, baseball was very

196

popular in Japan.

Post war, for some 40 years Japanese believed Americans to be a good brother. I think it was in the 1980's when Japanese economy was world No. 1, that opinions began to shift. Many Americans came to Japan to teach English, many Japanese came to America to expand their business.

この本で、幕末、黒船が初めて来た時に、日本人はアメリカについてとても深い興味を持ったことを述べました。

戦前、アメリカ文化は映画、ジャズ、小説、野球等、日本で本当に人気がありました。

戦後、40年間位数多くの日本人がアメリカ人は優れた兄貴であると信じていました。しかし日本経済が世界一の勢いがあった1980年代に意見が変わり始めました。数多くのアメリカ人が英語を教えるために日本へ来ましたし、数多くの日本人がビジネスの拡大の為にアメリカへ行きました。

Well I have written about the friction between Japanese and Americans in Japan. Basically, Japanese people have internal discipline. They can discipline themselves, while Americans cannot. It seems to me that Americans need to have discipline enforced from outside forces.

And this direct contact shifted people's opinions.

If I may say one thing, Americans have too much selfish ego. It is almost impossible to use an American in a job in Japan. They are way too demanding.

私は、日本における日本人とアメリカ人との交流の問題について書いています。基本的に、日本人は心の中に規律を持っていますから自己規制が出来ますが、アメリカ人は出来ません。やはりアメリカ人にも外部から強制された規律が必要です。

Chapter 4 After the War

　この直接の交流で、日本人の意見が変わりました。
　その一つが、アメリカ人はわがままで自我が強過ぎということでした。日本で、アメリカ人を仕事で使う事はほとんど不可能です。要求が有り過ぎるからです。

Now I am going to say something shocking here. I do not think that Americans understand the concept of Rights. Too many people think that by being born American, the Right to satisfaction is guaranteed. No it is not. The Right to attempt to achieve satisfaction is guaranteed. But nowhere is success guaranteed. Americans don't understand this fact. Americans have forgotten the part about working to achieve something.

　ここで、ショッキングな事を述べます。やはり、アメリカ人は権利ということを理解していません。数多くのアメリカ人は、ただアメリカ人に生まれただけで、満足する権利が保障されていると考えています。それは違います。確かに満足する為に努力する権利は保障されています。しかし、成功は約束されていないのです。いまのアメリカ人はその事が理解出来ていません。アメリカ人は一生懸命努力する事を忘れてしまっています。

Too many Americans, both in and out of Japan, virtually all Americans take an attitude to remake Japan, to make it more like America. This is the concept that Americans have of conversion. This is the belief that all nations of the world must convert to an American lifestyle. This comes out of American fear of countries that are different. Well until now, it was easy to find Japanese who worshiped America.

As I have said, no longer. Not only do average Americans in Japan, the English conversation teacher type behave badly, but

第 4 章　戦後

the lifestyle of the average American inside the United States is dropping to third world levels. What egoism for Americans to try and change Japanese society. Now Americans are no longer respected by Japanese. Japan has 2,600 years of history, ten times that of the United States.

　日本の中にいても、外にいても、ほとんどのアメリカ人は日本をもっとアメリカの様な国に作り直したいと考えています。これは全ての国がアメリカのライフスタイルに変わらなければならないとするアメリカ人の〝改宗〟の考え方です。この考え方はアメリカ人の、自分達とは違う国に対する恐れから来ます。まあ、現在まで、アメリカを崇拝している日本人を見つける事は簡単でした。
　ですが、今は違います。日本に居る普通のアメリカ人、英語の先生の様な人達が、とても態度が悪いだけでなく、アメリカにいる平均的アメリカ人の生活のレベルは第3世界のレベルにまで落ちました。そんなアメリカ人が日本社会を作り変えたい為に、自我を出し過ぎています。そんなアメリカ人は日本人から尊敬されなくなりました。日本は 2600 年の歴史が有ります。アメリカの 10 倍です。

Americans think that Japan is a naturally aggressive nation, that must be restrained by benevolent American power. There is a phrase in American English to describe America's relationship with Japan, "Finger in the collar". This is a very disrespectful attitude towards Japanese people.

May I remind you that the Edo Military government, which was toppled by the arrival of the Black ships, was actually 263 years of peace. Both internally and with all neighbors. Does American history have even one 10 year period when it was not involved in a war somewhere? I don't think so. These are some of the biggest

Chapter 4 After the War

reasons for Japanese disappointment in America.

　アメリカ人は、日本は元々攻撃的な国であると思っています。そして彼らは、アメリカが日本を抑えるべきであると思っています。アメリカ人の日米関係の気持ちを説明している、アメリカの英語のフレーズが有ります。それは、〝襟に指〟です。この意味は、アメリカ人の指を日本人の襟に入れているから、日本が他のアジアの国に攻撃する事を止めているということです。これは日本人を見下した意識です。

　アメリカ人に一つの真実を教えます。黒船の到着で潰された江戸幕府は軍事政府でした。しかし、軍事政府でも、263年間、平和でした。国内も他国との交流でも。アメリカは、自国の歴史で、10年間の戦争に関わっていない期間が有りますか？　無いでしょう。これらの理由で、日本人はだんだんアメリカについて落胆してきています。

　When I first arrived in Japan 40 years ago, it was a very egalitarian society. Almost all people were comfortably Middle Class. Thanks to some Japanese leading people accepting American ideas of predatory Capitalism, destruction of the Middle Class has just begun.

　It has become very difficult for Japanese people to achieve permanent employment after University. The only jobs available are low paying part time work.

　Men cannot get married.

　私が40年前に初めて日本へ来た時は、とても平等主義社会でした。ほとんどの日本人は中流階級でした。でも、何人かの指導的日本人がアメリカの略奪資本主義を導入して、それにより日本の中流階級の崩壊がいま始まっているのです。

　いまや大学を卒業しても、正社員の仕事を見つけることが困難

第４章　戦後

です。安いギャラのアルバイトしか有りません。
　しかも男性は結婚出来ません。

　Those America worshipping Japanese who are creating this echo what rich Americans say, "people don't work hard". Rich Corporate people in America use this excuse to pay very cheap wages. They say the reason people cannot live is not because wages are low, but workers are lazy. But the truth is, life is hard for most Americans.
　Maybe that is true in America, that some people do not work, but not Japan. Japanese workers are the most assiduous in the world. But income inequality in Japan is increasing. In America it is a disaster. The average American lives a miserable life of debt, with no possibility of changing it. And if Americans get sick, since America has no National Health Care, for most people the only option is bankruptcy or death.
　I really think Americans should wake up and see what their country has become.

　ここのアメリカ崇拝の日本人が1％の裕福なアメリカ人の言葉を繰り返しています。「人は一生懸命に働かない怠け者だ」。大金持ちのアメリカ企業の社長は安いギャラを払う為の言い訳に、この言葉を使います。彼らは、人々が生活が出来ないのはギャラが安いからでは無く、労働者が怠け者であることが理由だと言うのです。
　アメリカの場合、これは何人もの労働者がそうかも知れませんが、日本人は世界で最も根気強く勤勉な労働者です。でも、所得格差が増えています。アメリカではもう災害のレベルです。普通のアメリカ人は惨めな借金生活で、そこから抜け出すことが不可能です。それで、アメリカ人が病気になった場合、国民健康保険が無いから、選択は自己破産か死ぬかしか有りません。

Chapter 4 After the War

　やはりアメリカ人は目を覚まして、自分の国の真実を見るべき時に来ています。

And if I remember correctly, there was one famous American industrialist who treated his workers well. That was Henry Ford. When asked why he paid his workers such high wages, he replied with a joke, "If my workers do not have money, they cannot buy my cars."

　昔、アメリカで、自分の労働者に対して良い扱いをする実業家がいました。それはヘンリー・フォード氏でした。他の実業家から「何故あなたは労働者にそんなに高い給料を払うのか？」と問われた彼は「もし私の労働者が金を持っていなければ、私の工場で造った車を買うことが出来ないだろ」とジョークで返しました。

What the upper one percent of American society today does not realize is, if people cannot live, if they cannot buy a house, raise children, and have a decent life, the result will be left wing revolution.
And with the mega drought in the US now destroying American agriculture, this could bring Americans to a state of hopelessness, and left wing revolt. We need to be careful about this.

　アメリカの上位の１％が理解していない事は、もし国民が家を買えない、子供を育てる事が出来ない、普通の生活が出来ない、という状況が生み出すその結果は、左翼の革命だということです。
　そして、じわじわと進行しているアメリカの大干ばつによってアメリカの農産業が崩壊して、アメリカ国民が絶望状態となり、左翼革命が生じることも無きにしも非ずです。大いに注意が必要です。

Things to learn from Japanese people
日本人から学ぶこと

The President of the United States, in a recent April visit to Asia, committed a major blunder. There are many problems between Japan and South Korea. The President made an unequivocal statement in favor of South Korea on the Comfort Women issue. Well I have explained these issues in this book. The Koreans are very out of line, in some kind of fantasy world. And oh yes, South Korea STILL TODAY has government supervised prostitution centers for it's own military. Right now.

And America had a very successful Comfort Women system in Hawaii. The military also sponsored prostitution in the Philippines. Japan's system was 70 years ago. Is this really something that we should be fighting over? Well Americans today spend an awful lot of time fighting over social issues, like Gay marriage, or abortion rights.

　2014年4月のアジア訪問で、アメリカ大統領が大失敗を犯しました。日本と韓国の間には多くの問題があります。戦争の時の従軍慰安婦問題で、オバマ大統領は韓国に有利な明確な声明を出しました。この本で、私はこの問題を説明しています。この問題で韓国人は本当に悪い、何か空想の世界に居ます。そして、韓国政府は自国の軍隊の為の慰安所を<u>今でも</u>持っています。そう、現在でもあります。

　アメリカも戦争中にはハワイでかなり良い慰安婦システムがありました。また、アメリカ軍はフィリピンでも慰安所を作りました。日本のシステムは70年前の事です。現在の時代にその70年前の事で喧嘩するべきでしょうか？　現在のアメリカ人は社会問題の争い、例えばゲイの結婚、または中絶の権利のような争いに多く

203

Chapter 4 After the War

の時間をかけています。

  I imply that they are not important. They are not! There is a military word that I like from my studies. It is in German, the word is Schwerpunkt.

  A direct translation would be "heavy point". What it truly means is to concentrate one's forces at a vital point of the enemy front line, and achieve strategic breakthrough.

  For both Japan and America, we are going to have to concentrate our efforts on what is important. That is not social issues like Gay marriage, abortion, or what was the Japanese Comfort Women system of 70 years ago.

　私はそれらは大切なことでは無いと言いたい。大切ではありません！　私の研究で、好きな軍事の言葉が有ります。それはドイツ語の〝Schwerpunkt〟です。

　直訳すると、〝重い点〟です。本当の意味は、自分の部隊を敵の前線の重要な所に集中して、戦略的な突破をすることです。

　日本とアメリカ両国はこれから、大切な事に集中しなければなりません。ゲイの結婚、中絶の権利、70年前の日本の慰安婦システムについての争いは、大切なことではありません。

  Americans are finally noticing the weather is changing. Well in Japan, we have known this for a long time. It is about to become deadly. For a lot of people. In America, you are about to lose the United States west of the Mississippi river. The Ogallala reservoir is nearly over. It cannot be replaced. Goodbye to agriculture in the Great Plains states. This year the California drought is finally making headlines. But it has always been there. This year the impacts on agriculture will be enormous.

California produces 2/3rds of America's fruits and vegetables. A large portion of that will no longer be available. Then, the prices of beef, pork, and chicken will rise dramatically. In a worst case scenario they will double in 2014. And this is a semipermeant condition that will quickly get worse. There is no food or water for animals. The Colorado river is forecast to disappear in 10 years. Think I am joking? Look it up in Google. The United States is shifting to desert because of man made climate change. All climate scientists agree with my dire assessment.

　やっと、アメリカ人が気候の変化に気付いてきています。日本では何年も前からこういう事に気付いていました。これから、気候の変化が原因で多くの人が死ぬでしょう。アメリカでは、ミシシッピ川より西の地域を間もなく失うでしょう。オガララ帯水層はほとんど水を取れない状態になっています。そこに再び水を入れる事は不可能です。そして、アメリカの大草原の州では農産業が終わり、人間も住めません。カリフォルニアの干ばつはやっと新聞の見出しに載るようになりました。しかし、この干ばつは昔からあり、今年のアメリカの農産業に甚大な影響を与えるでしょう。

　カリフォルニアではアメリカの果物と野菜の３分の２を生産しています。その大部分はもう無くなるでしょう。そうなると、牛肉、豚肉、鶏肉の価格が、急激に上がります。最悪のシナリオでは2014年時点で倍になります。この気候の変化、温暖化は半永久的なもので、これから酷くなるしかありません。その時には農産業や動物に使える、水や餌は無くなるでしょう。コロラド川は10年以内に消えるという予想があります。もしもこれが嘘だと思うようでしたら、グーグルで探してみて下さい。人間が作った温暖化でアメリカ合衆国は砂漠化が進行しています。全ての気候科学者は私の恐ろしい評価と一致しています。

Chapter 4 After the War

  I think it is time for Americans to learn from Japanese society how to survive. It is time to cease being a nation of self centered egoists, and learn true social cooperation. And what will be the inevitable result of rich Americans, and rich Japanese increasing their wealth through income inequality?

  Well, notice I am saying that Climate change is destroying agriculture. That means no food for people without hope of a decent life because of income inequality. The result is Left Wing revolution.

  やはり、これからアメリカ人は日本人から生き残る方法を学ぶべきです。自分の事ばかり考えている利己主義者の国から、社会的な協力が出来る国民になるべきです。それでは、数人の日本人、アメリカ人が収入格差でお金持ちになると、必然的にどのような結果が出るでしょうか？

  まあ、私は温暖化が農産業を崩壊させていると述べました。それは、良い生活の望みがない人には、食料も無いという意味です。その結果は左翼革命です。

  In America, the "Occupy" movement is still there, but very underground, like a smoldering fire. When they were prominent in the news a few years ago, I was surprised. It was very left wing, just like the major protest movement that swept America during the Vietnam war. In fact, a lot of the same people of the Vietnam war era Left appeared out of hiding, and schooled the younger ones in revolutionary tactics. In Japan and America, we cannot be complacent, this is a recipe for revolution.

  アメリカでは、〝ウォール街を占拠せよ〟の運動は今でもあります。くすぶっている火のように潜行的な運動となっています。数年前に、その運動がニュースで目立った時に、私は驚きました。

とても左翼的で、ベトナム戦争の抗議運動と同じでした。実はこの時、アメリカ・ベトナム戦争時代の左派の人が表に出て来て、その〝ウォール街を占拠せよ〟の若者に革命の戦術を教えました。これは左翼革命のレシピです。日本人もアメリカ人もひとりよがりな事をやっている時ではありません。

What will be the future for America? I am afraid it will be hard times. Food and water shortages will dominate the national conversation. And I expect they will get rapidly worse. I have commented on American selfishness, and desire for gratification. Well, I am afraid those will become fatal traits. Americans need to understand that people who will survive in the future are going to be those who can work with others, who can compromise and cooperate.

アメリカの将来はどのようなものでしょうか？　たぶん厳しく、苦しい時代になるでしょう。国の話題は水不足、食料不足になります。この問題は急速に酷くなるだろうというのが私の予測です。私はアメリカ人の利己主義、自己満足の為の欲求について述べてきましたが、これからの時代、それは致命的な特徴になるだろうと危惧しています。未来において生き残る人は、他人と協力が出来る人、妥協を出来る人だということをアメリカ人は理解しなくてはいけません。

What will survive in the 21st century might be local communities. In the communities, they will need a water supply, and ability to grow enough food. Doctors, soldiers, farmers and carpenters will become very important people. There will be little need for lawyers, and no need at all for real estate agents or lifestyle consultants. No Corporate CEO's either, the military

Chapter 4 After the War

people will take care of management. Military people will know how to organize people and motivate them.

I think that most of these surviving communities will be east of the Mississippi river. There is just not going to be enough water west of the river, except in western Washington and Oregon. The land west of the Mississippi will be deep desert. Like the present Sahara desert.

　21世紀に生き残るのは小さいコミュニティーかもしれません。その時は、そこには水源と住んでいる人たちが食べられる食料を生産する土地が必要です。医者、兵士、農家、大工は大切な人になります。弁護士はそんなに必要無いでしょう。不動産屋、生活コンサルタントは要りません。企業の取締役はもう必要無いです。そのコミュニティーの管理については、軍人が上手いでしょう。管理された軍人は人を組織すること、人々をやる気にさせる事が上手いです。
　将来、この生き残るコミュニティーのほんとどはミシシッピ川の東側になるでしょう。ミシシッピ川の西側には、ワシントン州とオレゴン州の西部以外に、人が生きる為の水の量は足りなくなるでしょう。ミシシッピ川の西側のアメリカは深い砂漠になるかもしれません。現在のサハラ砂漠の様に。

I say this because if we ignore these drastic climate changes, as water sources disappear from the U.S., food disappears and there could be too much mass movement of people. Right now, the Federal government is not handling the issue efficiently. Definitely, it will be hard and difficult times.

For the same reason, Chinese are desperate to secure water sources worldwide. China has the same problem with drought as the U.S. However, China does understand the present situation better.

何故こういう事を書くかというと、現在続いている激しい気候変動を無視し続けるとアメリカから水源が消え、食料が消え、数多くのアメリカ人が難民になることすら有り得るからです。現在、アメリカ連邦政府はこの問題を処理する事が出来ません。このままではアメリカの未来は厳しい、つらい時代になります。

中国人が世界中で水源の確保に躍起になっているのはこのせいなのです。中国もアメリカと同じ課題を抱えているのです。その点、アメリカより中国の方が現実が見えているのかも知れません。

A letter to Korea
韓国への手紙

I have one word for my Korean friends. Why? Why have you made such a mess? Things were going so well between Korea and Japan. There was a great boom in interest among Japanese people in Korean language and culture. Many young Koreans became stars and celebrities on Japanese television.

Then activists started this international movement about erecting statues to the Comfort Women, and screaming all around the world how terrible Japan is. The sad fact is, they are screaming about events that did not happen. They just made it up. And now Koreans are surprised that Japanese tourists no longer visit Korea and spend money there. And not only are you insulting Japan in many countries around the world, in your own country, you are insulting yourselves.

私の韓国の友達に一つの事を尋ねたいです。何故？　何故こんなにひどい状態をあなた達は作ったのですか？　日韓の関係は本当によくなっていたのに。3年前まで、日本で韓国の文化、韓国

Chapter 4 After the War

語は大人気でした。数多くの韓国の若者が日本のテレビでタレント、スターになりました。
　その後、活動家が、世界のどこでも〝従軍慰安婦記念碑〟を作ったり、日本が酷い国であると叫んだりして国際的な運動を始めました。悲しい事実は、彼らは存在が無かった出来事について叫んでいる、勝手な想像で作られているということです。そのことで、日本人観光客がもう韓国へ訪問しない、韓国でお金を落とさないという事に韓国人が驚いています。そして、世界の国々で日本に対して失礼なことを言っているだけではなく、自分の国でも自分自身に対して失礼なことをしています。

Beating university professors who have investigated the Comfort women's claim, is sacrilege. I thought teachers were the highest people in Korean society, When thugs beat and humiliated a Seoul university professor, you debased your society and yourselves.

A department store in Japan selling Korean products and souvenirs during the Korean culture boom (Bankrupt in April 2014)
韓流ブームで韓国の品物を販売していた日本のデパートです
（2014 年 4 月経営破綻）

第4章　戦後

He had studied the Comfort Women issue, and concluded that their testimony was unreliable. He also said that the Japanese annexation period was not so bad. For this he was beaten and humiliated in public, forced to bow in apology to the Comfort Women.

　韓国で元慰安婦を研究した大学の教授が殴られた事件は冒涜です。韓国の社会で大学教授は一番偉い人でしょう？　暴漢がソウル大学の教授を殴った時に、彼は自分自身と韓国社会の品格を落としました。この教授が慰安婦問題を研究して、彼女達の証言は信用出来ないという結論を出しました。彼も日本の併合はそんなにひどくなかったと言いました。この声明の為に、この教授は人前で暴漢に殴られ、強制的に元慰安婦に謝罪をさせられました。

A 95 year old Korean man was killed in the park by a Korean man in his 30's. He was sentenced to a few years in jail, but the court said it could understand the feeling of the young man, the old man insulted Korea.

I also thought old people were respected. It was that way when I lived in Korea 38 years ago. But it is no longer true.

　ある公園で95歳の男性が30代の男性に殺されました。犯人はわずか数年の懲役を受けました。裁判官は犯人の気持ちを理解することが出来ると言い、95歳の男性こそが韓国に失礼だという判決を言いわたしました。

　私は韓国社会ではお年寄りが尊敬されていると思っていました。私が38年前に、韓国に住んだ時はそうでした。しかし、いまやそうではありません。

Middle aged Koreans ignore their own parents. Grandmothers have to sell their bodies in Jongmyo Park in Seoul. They are

Chapter 4 After the War

called Bacchus ladies, because they also sell the Bacchus energy drink.

And despite the fact, why do Koreans keep on wailing about the Comfort Women issue of 70 years ago and accusing Japan of crimes that did not happen? The truth is it the shame of Koreans that they sold their own daughters, so they Koreans try to hide it. Koreans have falsely accused the Japanese military of forcefully abducting young girls to Comfort Women stations to cover up what they themselves did. This itself, is a crime.

現在、中年の韓国人は自分の親を無視しています。多くのおばあさんたちがソウルの宗廟公園で生活の為に売春を行なっていました。彼らはバッカスエナジー飲料も売っていたので、バッカスレディーと呼ばれていました。

にも拘わらず何故、韓国人は70年前の慰安婦問題を日本に文句を言うのですか？ それは韓国人社会の闇そのものであり自分の娘を本人に内緒で女衒に売りとばした事実を覆い隠そうとする

Seoul's Tsunami shaped unusual new city hall
ソウルの津波形の異常な新市庁舎です

出典：Rocket News24「The unfortunate implications of Seoul's tsunami-shaped City Hall」（2013年11月7日）

第4章　戦後

ものです。その様にして売られた女性の中には親が自分を売ったとは知らず、強制的に日本軍の慰安所に連れていかれたと思っている人がいるのです。日本は完全な濡れ衣を着せられています。

Now Korea has distorted it's own past so greatly, and debases it's own culture to support a fantasy. You are killing yourselves as far as I can see, you have become an abnormal society.

　現在の韓国は自国の歴史を歪曲して伝え、空想を支持する為に自分の文化の品格を落としています。韓国人は自分自身を殺しているとさえ私には見えます。その行動は常軌を逸しており異常です。もう人間ではなく、怪物になりました。

A couple of years ago, a new city hall was built in Seoul. The old one was built during the period of Japanese annexation. The plan was to tear it down and build a new one, but many people in Korea objected.
So a new city hall was built behind the old one. It is in the shape of a Tsunami engulfing the old Japanese built city hall. I find this highly disturbing, and indicative that something is seriously mentally wrong with Korean people. I have read that when Japan's disastrous 2011 earthquake struck, many Koreans publicly rejoiced. This is not the action of a civilized people.

　数年前に、ソウルで新しい市庁舎が建てられました。古い市庁舎は日韓併合時代に建てられたものです。計画は古い市庁舎を解体して、新しい建物を建てる事でした。しかし数多くの韓国人が歴史的な建物を解体する事に反対でした。
　それで、古い市庁舎の裏に、新しい市庁舎が建てられました。新しい建物は、古い日韓併合時代の建物を巻き込む津波の形に造られました。これは本当に不穏なことです。やはり韓国人は精神

213

Chapter 4 After the War

的な病気です。2011年3月11日の東日本大震災で、公式に喜んだ韓国人が多かったということをニュースで読みました。文明人の反応としては問題があります。

Many Americans believe that they are at war with Islam. I do not agree with this either, but many Americans think so because of the 2001 attack in New York City. They regard Iran as an enemy country. Again, I do not agree. However, if a major earthquake happens in Iran, and many people die and are injured, Americans do not rejoice in their misery and tragedy. They do not build buildings or monuments celebrating the misfortune of Iranian people.

What is wrong with Koreans?

一方、数多くのアメリカ人が自分の国がイスラムと戦争中であると信じています。私は同意しないけれど、2001年のニューヨーク市で起きたテロ事件で、アメリカ人はイランを敵の国であると思っています。これにも私は同意しません。しかし、イランで大地震が起こって、数多くの人が死んだり負傷した場合は、アメリカ人はイラン人の苦しんでいる姿や悲劇を喜びません。イラン人の不幸を祝う記念碑を造りません。

韓国人はどうしてこんなに非常識で不道徳なのでしょうか？

Recently, you have suffered a terrible disaster, in the Sewol ferry disaster where 284 people died. But shamefully, the Captain, instead of helping the passengers, was one of the first to leave the ship. And it seems that the overloading of cargo and passengers beyond safety limits is normal procedure in Korea. In Japan, people were glued to their television sets during the disaster, people were very worried about the young children trapped in the ferry.

　最近、とてもひどい災害が有りました。セウォル号のフェリー沈没、284人死亡です。しかし、船長は最初に船から逃げました。乗客を助けるよりも、自分の命が大切でした。この事故から分かったことは、韓国社会では貨物、乗客を乗せ過ぎることは日常的で普通の行為だったということです。この時、日本人は皆、韓国の子供達を心配し家族に同情しました。

　In 2003, a fire was set by an arsonist in a subway station in Daegu. The engineer panicked and locked people in the train, killing 198. In 1995 the Sampoong Department Store collapsed. The building was of very sub standard construction. On the day of the collapse, cracks opened in the upper floors, up to 10 cm wide. The executives abandoned the building, but did not order an evacuation because of the large number of customers inside. They did not want to lose the day's profit, that was more important than people's lives. The collapse killed 502 people.

　2003年に、大邱市の地下鉄の駅で放火された火災が起きました。運転手がパニックをおこし、乗客のいる電車の扉をロックして逃げ198人が亡くなりました。1995年にソウルの三豊百貨店が崩壊しました。建物の工事は建築法の基準以下でしたので、崩壊の日、上の階で10センチのひびが入り、役員達は建物から逃げました。しかし、お客さんの数が多かったので、避難命令を出しませんでした。人の命より、利益が大切だったのです。崩壊で502人が亡くなりました。

　Perhaps instead of wandering the countries of the world with all these false accusations about Japan, you should try and reform your own society?

Chapter 4 After the War

And more and more countries will tire about your complaints about Japan. All right, most people today don't know clearly what happened in WWII. But soon people will be saying, "Oh No! Here come those Koreans! All they ever do is complain how terrible Japan was to them 70 years ago. They want us to punish Japan for them. Can't they do anything for themselves?"

　おそらく、世界の国々を回って、日本が悪いと嘘の告発をするより、自分の国の社会を作り直した方が良いのではないでしょうか？

　そのことで、だんだん様々な国の人々が、韓国が発する日本への文句に疲れています。まあ、世界のほとんどの人は第二次世界大戦でどういう事が有ったかを知りません。しかし、徐々に色々な人が「まったく！また韓国人が来ました！いつも日本が70年前に酷かったという文句ばかりで、自分達の代わりに、私たちの為に日本を罰して下さいと言っている。やはり韓国は自分では何も出来ない国ですね！」と言うようになりました。

Look at Vietnam. Vietnam fought a 30 year war for freedom from France and America. Did you ever fight a war against Japan? No, you did not. Granted, you had exiles in various countries asking for foreign help against Japan, but in Korea itself, the Resistance movement never had more than about 1,500 guerrillas in the far north. They were afraid to approach a farmer for food even in the remotest villages. That means they did not have popular support.

In Vietnam, during both the wars against the French and the Americans, guerrilla soldiers could always find support from the populace, even right next to foreign bases. No such movement existed in Korea.

216

第 4 章　戦後

　ベトナムを考えて下さい。ベトナムは自分達の自由の為にフランス、アメリカと 30 年間戦争を戦いました。韓国が日本と戦争をした事が有りますか？　いいえ、した事が有りません。色々な国々で、助けを求める亡命者がいましたが、当時朝鮮の中では、満州の国境近くにレジスタンス運動のゲリラが 1,500 人位いた程度でした。その人達は、遠く離れている村でも、食料の為に農家に近づくことすら怖がっていました。それは、そのゲリラは当時朝鮮人から支持されていなかったということです。

　ベトナムで、フランス、アメリカの両方に対する戦争で、ゲリラは常に国民から支持があり、その外国の基地のすぐ隣であっても支持がありました。そのようなゲリラ運動は、当時朝鮮では全くありませんでした。

And the French and Americans devastated Vietnam. Towns and villages were destroyed. Defoliants still give people cancers today. For example, many Siamese twines are born into Vietnamese families.

Yet Vietnam is seeking to join a trade pact with America. They do not simply keep crying about the past, saying help me. They work hard to help themselves. The Vietnamese people are people of respect.

　フランス軍、アメリカ軍はベトナムを破壊しました。村も街も破壊されました。アメリカが利用した枯れ葉剤で沢山の哀れなシャム双生児が誕生し、現在でもそれが原因で癌になる人が多くいます。

　それでも、現在ベトナムはアメリカと貿易協定を結ぶ努力をしています。過去の事を叫ぶことばかりしないで、私達を助けてということばかり言わないで、自分達で頑張っています。ベトナム国民は尊敬出来る人たちです。

Chapter 4 After the War

What is wrong with Korea? To act with proper pride is the way of an intelligent person. Do not always hold a grudge against another, or constantly demand compensation, this is not good. Until Korea has freedom of speech, you will always be a third class country.

韓国の問題は何ですか？ もっと誇りある行動を取るのが知性を持つ者の行為です。それは相手を恨むことでも相手にたかることでもありません。韓国の人は言論の自由化をしない限り三流国であるということを恥じないといけません。

A note to China
中国へのノート

I do have some idea why you keep bashing Japan. I think there are two reasons.

One, is to try to ensure that China, not Japan will become the leader of Asia. The other is that the Chinese government is terrified of social unrest leading to revolution, so this is why China takes such an anti Japan stance. China today has great income inequality, and the pollution is terrible. You are running out of energy to support your present society. Attacking Japan gives your people something else to think about.

私は中国が日本バッシングを行なっている理由を理解しています。それは二つ有ります。

１つはアジアのリーダーは日本ではなく、中国だと決める事です。もう１つの理由は、中国政府が革命につながる社会混乱を恐れて民衆の不満のエネルギーを日本へ向けさせる為です。現在の中国は、とても所得格差が大きく、公害も酷いです。現在の社会

を守るエネルギーも有りません。日本をバッシングすれば、中国国民の注目を違う方に向けることが出来ます。

　I have written a little bit about how drought is affecting the United States. China has the same drought problems. Therefore, you need to cooperate with Japan, we have many top class scientists. No, unfortunately we cannot save you,. No, we cannot save you, you are too big. But Japan is a natural partner of China. You should stop attacking us and look for ways we can cooperate. Japan can help alleviate some of your serious problems, we would like to do so.

　In any case, the Chinese people are very resilient. Unlike American civilization, Chinese culture will survive no matter what hardships occur.

　私は、干ばつがアメリカでどう影響を及ぼしているかという事を少し述べていますが、中国も同じように厳しい干ばつ問題があります。だから、中国は優れた科学技術を持つ日本と協力する必要があります。残念ながら、私たちは中国を救う事は出来ません、中国は大き過ぎます。だからこそ中国は日本を攻撃するのではなく、協力する方法を探るべきです。日本は誠意をもって中国の深刻な問題を軽減する事が出来るだろうと思います。

　いずれにしても、中国人は強い回復力が有ります。アメリカ文明とは違って、どんな困難が起こっても、中国文化は残るでしょう。

Chapter 4 After the War

Japan and the future
日本と将来

The very most important thing for Japan is to increase food self sufficiency. TPP is an absolute mistake. The funny thing about TPP is, even though American agricultural corporations are screaming for access to Japanese markets, in a few short years they will not have enough food to feed their own people. American agriculture has many problems. In a few years, American agriculture production will decline greatly. I do think that many people around the world will starve as American agriculture disappears. But Japan will survive as a society, and a civilization. This is because Japanese people are hard working, not selfish, and do not complain.

I know, such selfish Japanese have increased over the years, I have seen it. I think it is too much admiration of what passes for American culture, an idea that you can concentrate on self gratification. But we can now see where American cultural themes of self gratification is leading them, and that is to destruction. The United States of America should make a good case study of how NOT to run a country.

まず日本にとって最も大切な事は食料自給率を上げる事です。TPPは絶対に間違いです。TPPのおかしなところは、アメリカの農産業の企業が強気で日本市場の支配を要求していることです。ですが、数年後にはアメリカ人自身を養うだけの食糧が確保出来るのか、アメリカ農業には多くの課題が有ります。数年後、アメリカの農産業が衰退している可能性があります。その時には世界で餓死する人も居るでしょう。しかし、日本は社会として、文明として大丈夫だと思います。何故なら、日本人は利己的ではなく

一生懸命に働き、不満を言わないからです。
　とは言え、私は、ここのところ利己的な日本人が増えている事を知っています。やはりアメリカ文化、自分の欲望を満たすことだけを考える自己満足に魅了されていることが原因でしょう。でも、現在のアメリカが自己満足の文化でどうなっているかを見ることが出来、それは破壊にあるということ、現在のアメリカは、国の運営を間違っていることがよく分かります。

The second thing that Japan should do is to begin the fight against Global Warming. America refuses to take leadership here. In any case, America will soon have too much domestic chaos to be a reliable partner. So Japan and Europe should do it. The fight will have two aspects. One, we must absolutely get away from fossil fuels. Alternatives must be found.

The second aspect is Geo Engineering. We are going to have to modify the climate of the planet, so that human civilization can survive. Otherwise, it is likely that the human race will become extinct in 100 years. In this, I expect that Russia, European countries, and even China could be good partners. However, America still cannot even decide if it is real. I suggest that we encourage the immigration of qualified American scientists to Japan.

　その次に日本がやるべき事は、未来の地球を救う為に温暖化と戦う事です。アメリカはこの問題でリーダーシップを取ることを拒否しています。とにかく、アメリカは将来来る国内の混乱でパートナーにはなりません。だから、日本と欧州が行なうべきです。この戦いには二つの側面が有ります。一つ目は、絶対に化石燃料を諦めて、代わりの燃料を見つけなければならないことです。
　二つ目は、二酸化炭素を減らして地球の空気を作り直す事です。そうしないと、100年後には人類は壊滅的な打撃を受ける可能性

Chapter 4 After the War

が有ります。この戦いでは、ロシア、ヨーロッパの国々、中国でも良きパートナーになります。しかし、アメリカはまだ温暖化が本当に存在するかどうかを決定する事さえ出来ていません。私はアメリカの気象科学者を日本へ招聘(しょうへい)すべきだと思います。

The American shale oil boom is near collapse. It is facing diminishing returns. It just costs too much to get it out of the ground. In any case, since it takes 3 barrels of water to get 1 barrel of oil by fracking, it will soon become impossible. Because of drought, aquifers have been depleted, there is no water.

America talks of a Global Standard. What this really means is American standard. But lack of fuel will make this impossible. We will see a return to regionalism across the world. Oil as a fuel will gradually become impossible. And I think the sailing ship will come back. Why not? Wind power is free, does not pollute and cause Global Warming. It will take longer to travel between countries, but why not? People may think I am kidding here, but this is serious. We need to develop alternatives to fossil fuels as soon as possible.

アメリカのシェールオイルは崩壊に近いです。徐々に採れなくなっています。採掘する為のコストがかかり過ぎるのです。とにかく、フラッキングで原油を１バレル取る為に、３バレルの水が必要ですから、まもなく不可能になります。何故ならアメリカは干ばつ続きで、地下水が不足しているからです。

アメリカ人はグローバル・スタンダードという事を言います。この言葉の本当の意味はアメリカの基準です。でも燃料の欠乏で将来的には不可能になる可能性があります。世界のあちらこちらで、地方自治的に主体は国家レベルではなく地域レベルになる可能性もあります。将来、石油はもう燃料として利用する事が不可能になるでしょう。だから私は、帆船を再び使うことになること

を望んでいます。私の個人的希望です。風力は無料で、公害も出さないし、温暖化の原因にはなりません。海外への旅行は今より時間がかかるけれど、良いでしょう（笑）。冗談はさて置くとして、早く化石燃料に代わるエネルギーの開発を急がねばなりません。

In the future, Japan should be more proactive in Asia, a true leader in many areas. One of these areas is space exploration. Japan, in league with other nations, should colonize Mars. We in Japan should begin a future that will give the human race a great destiny. While we must maintain the earth, for our children, we should expand into space.

日本はこれより、アジアで強いリーダーとなるべきです。その一つに宇宙探査があります。日本は他の国と協力しながら、火星に基地を造るべきです。日本から、人類に素晴らしい運命を与える未来を始めるべきです。地道な大地の維持と未来を築く宇宙への挑戦を子供たちに示していかなくてはいけません。

To sum it up
最後に

There are going to be those people who get very emotional, that will say this book is a whitewash of history. They will again scream about how bad Japan was. In particular, the Japanese masochists will scream. Well, perhaps post war, such thinking was necessary for Japan to survive. If Americans had suspected that Japan was not submissive post war, they would have done something terrible to Japan. So perhaps we can say that it was necessary for a time to have masochistic Japanese people. But

Chapter 4 After the War

that time is now over, Japan is an independent country.

　理性が欠けた感情論者の何人かがこの本は歴史の虚偽だと言うでしょう。その人たちは日本人が酷い人種と叫びます。特に、マゾヒスチックな日本人ほどそう叫びます。もしかしたら、戦後、日本が生き残るために、そのような考え方は必要だったかもしれません。もし戦後にアメリカ人が日本人を従順ではないと思っていたら、日本に恐ろしい事をしたでしょう。だから、日本人の自虐性は当時は必要悪だったのかもしれません。しかし、もう日本は独立国です。その必要はありません。

One of my points with this book is to point that Americans were not so good in the field either. They depend too much upon massive firepower. In fact, all in all, I must say that the Japanese soldier was better behaved, more disciplined. Americans just don't have discipline, and outside their country, they behave badly. That is still true today.

It is time for America to stop fighting WWII in their hearts. The war is long over, America did win.

　この本の一つのポイントは、アメリカ兵はあまり戦争の戦い方は上手ではなかったということです。彼らは大規模な火力に頼り過ぎています。それから正直に言うと、全体で考えると、昔の日本兵はアメリカ兵より規律は良かったです。アメリカ人は規律が無く、アメリカ以外の国での振舞いが悪いです。それは現在でも同じです。

　アメリカ人はもう大東亜戦争を心の中で戦うことをやめるべきです。戦争は昔のことで、アメリカは勝ちました。

And if I were to go through the news, I am sure I could find some outrageous remark by an American State Governor, or Congress person. Something like "Black people benefited from slavery because it brought them to America." You can hear that comment a lot in America these days. It is an extremely insensitive comment. So why all the screaming when the mayor of some city or other in Japan makes a remark about Nanking? It is because some Americans desire to attack Japan for any reason.

　もし、私がニュースを探したら、どこかの州知事、議員の許し難い話を見つける事が出来るでしょう。例えば、「アメリカ黒人にとって奴隷時代は良かった、何故なら、奴隷制でアメリカへ来るチャンスが有ったから」。その話は現在のアメリカでごく普通に語られています。何とも無神経な話です。それでも何故か、どこかの日本の地方議員や市長が南京について話をすると、外国のマスコミは爆発します。その裏に〝何か〟の意思が働いているからです。

In particular with social cooperation, I think there is much that America could learn from Japan. But I don't think Americans will. Individual ego is too great. Perhaps in another 20 or 30 years, after a time of great tribulation, the American character might change to something better.

And with yearly drought destroying America's agriculture in the near future, I think that time has come. I think one immediate thing America could do to help prevent internal disorder would be to reinstate the draft. And for people who physically do not qualify for the military, put them in Civil Service. Everybody serves, no exceptions. Those who refuse to serve will not be issued with food. Simple. But it would help to restore a sense of community. This is not at all Communism. America is going to have to develop a society based on cooperation like Japan has.

　社会的な協力について、アメリカ人は日本から学んだ方が良い

Chapter 4 After the War

でしょう。しかしアメリカ人はそうしません。アメリカ人の自我は強過ぎます。もしかしたら、20年か30年後、苦しみの時代があってから、アメリカ人の性格が少し良くなるかも知れません。

　毎年の干ばつでアメリカの農産業は近い将来崩壊して、混乱の時代が訪れるだろうと私は感じています。その時の混乱を予防する為に、アメリカが即座に出来る事は徴兵を復活する事だと私は思います。そして肉体的に軍に向かない人は公務員にすれば良いでしょう。全員が国の為に働き、例外は無しです。国の為に働かない人には食料を渡しません。でも、これでコミュニティーの意識がアメリカに戻るでしょう。だからと言って共産主義を説いている訳ではありません。日本の様な支え合い、よく働く国民になるべきと言っているのです。

In Japan, we have the Imperial Household, something all Japanese can identify with. There is really no such equivalent in America, talking about the Constitution is too vague. Today's Americans really don't understand what it means, they do not understand the difference between rights and privileges.

　日本には皇室があります。全ての日本人が皇室と一体感を持つ事が出来ます。アメリカにはその様な価値のあるものが有りません。憲法について話すことも漠然としています。それどころか、現在のアメリカ人には憲法の意味すら分からない人が多く、権利と特権の違いが分かりません。

I do hope that the America of my birth can somehow get it together. And survive as a nation. But you do not have much time. My guess is two or three years before chaos overtakes you.

　私は祖国アメリカが何とかうまくやることを望んでいます。国として生き残る事を望んでいます。しかし、地球規模的時間があ

りません。私の推測では、アメリカが初期の混乱に陥るまでは後２、３年しか有りません。

終わりに

Epilogue

Epilogue

I still remember the first day I arrived in Japan. I had anticipated this day since the age of 12. This was the age when I first began to think as an adult. I read a biography of General Yamashita Tomoyuki. At the end of the book, there was a letter he wrote to son, just before his execution. Of course, the execution sentence was totally unfair. An American would write about how terrible the sentence was, how unjust.

General Yamashita wrote no such thing. He told his son that the duty to lead the family now fell upon him, he would have to take care of his mother and siblings. I was surprised. What a noble man he was. I wondered, what kind of country could produce such a man? This was the beginning of my fascination with Japan.

今でも、最初に日本へ来た日を覚えています。12歳から、この日を期待していました。これは私が大人として考え始めた歳でした。この歳に日本帝国陸軍山下奉文大将の伝記を読みました。その本の最後に、処刑される直前に、彼が息子さんへ書いた手紙がありました。勿論、その死刑判決は不当でした。アメリカ人の場合なら、その最後の手紙では判決は酷い、不当であるという事ばかり書きます。しかし山下大将はその様な事を書きませんでした。

彼は、息子にこれから家族の大黒柱として生きる義務があり、これから母と兄弟の面倒を見る必要があると、そう書きました。私は驚きました。なんと高潔な人でしょう。どの様な国で、この様な素晴らしい人が生まれ育つことが出来るのだろう？これが私の日本に対する魅力のきっかけでした。

When I first came, I was a new Marine, and I came to Iwakuni, Yamaguchi Prefecture. When I walked outside the gate of the US base, I felt an immediate sense of belonging. I knew that Japan was my place, my home. It was a very mysterious feeling.

Even though I could not yet speak Japanese, I could immediately understand what people were doing by watching them perform their everyday lives.

　最初に日本へ来た時、私は新米の海兵隊員で、山口県岩国基地に来ました。アメリカの基地の門を出て、外の日本の街を歩くと、すぐに日本への帰属意識を感じました。地球上で、日本が私の場所で、私の永住の地であると、すぐに分かりました。それは実に不思議な感覚でした。まだ日本語が出来なくても、日本人の日常生活の行ないを見て、何をしているのか理解することが出来ました。

As I gradually learned Japanese, I learned how Japanese society functioned. It was so well ordered compared to the America in which I had been born.

And unlike in America, people worked hard, and took a deep pride in what they did. Well, of course in America people do work hard, and many do take pride in their work. But Japanese people have an intensity about what they do, they go into much more detail about things than Americans.

　徐々に日本語を覚えて、日本の社会はどのように機能するかを学びました。それは、私が生まれ育ったアメリカと比較して、とても秩序がありました。

　それと、アメリカとは違い、人々は一生懸命に働いて、自分の仕事に誇りを持っていました。まあ、勿論、一生懸命に働いて、自分の仕事に誇りを持っているアメリカ人も居ます。しかし、日本人はそんなアメリカ人よりも更に自分達の仕事に熱心で、繊細でした。

And Japanese society functions on harmony. In America, with

Epilogue

other people, they are always constantly trying to prove that they are better than everyone else.

In Japan, even people of great ability, are modest about their accomplishments. I found this to be very admirable. From the first day I arrived, I knew I would live in Japan forever. For me, it is the most perfect place in the world.

　日本の社会において、和は大切です。アメリカでは、人はいつも他人と競争して、自分が他人より優れているということを証明しようとしています。日本では、優れた能力がある人でも、自分の成果について自慢しません。
　このような考え方はとても魅力的でした。最初に日本に来た日から、私は永遠に日本で生きるだろうと感じました。私にとって日本は、この世の中で一番完璧な所と映りました。

We are about to enter a new phase in the Japanese/American relationship. The first phase was, from the arrival of Commodore Perry to the end of WWII. This phase was marked by increasing American efforts to contain Japan. And America applied continuous pressure on Japan which eventually forced Japan to go to war for self defense.

The second phase was from the end of the war until now. This phase has been marked by American dominance of the world. Despite American continued distrust of Japan, Japan has remained a loyal supporter of American policy.

　さて、今日の日米関係はいま、新たな段階に入ろうとしています。第1段階は、ペリー提督の来日から大東亜戦争の終結まででした。この段階では、アメリカが徐々に日本を封じ込めようとしました。アメリカは継続的に日本に圧力をかけたため、日本はその存在を守る為に自存自衛の戦争を開始する選択しかありません

でした。
　第2段階は終戦から現在までです。この段階では、アメリカが世界を支配していました。日本に対するアメリカの不信が続いていても、日本は忠実にアメリカ政策を支持してきました。

Phase three is about to begin. From now, America will be increasingly weakened by internal disorders. The American financial system, agriculture, and shale oil are all nearing collapse. In the future, America will need Japan as a strong partner in Asia, as America will no longer be able to project power as in the post WWII period. And this is why I think it is important for Americans to cease bashing Japan over WWII issues.

The truth is, Japan was certainly not the evil Empire that people thought it was. And America itself was not the great moral country in WWII that some Americans like to believe. Americans are going to have to learn the truth of history.

For America in the near future, Japanese goodwill and cooperation will essential for America. And I have to say, Americans should make more effort to keep that goodwill. And then both countries shall be able to face the future together, in partnership.

　第3段階は間もなく始まります。これから、アメリカは徐々に国内の混乱により弱くなります。アメリカの金融経済、農産業、シェールオイルは全て崩壊が近づいています。これからアメリカはアジアの強いパートナーとして日本が必要です。アメリカはもう大東亜戦争後の時代の様に、世界中に戦力を展開出来ません。これが、アメリカ人が大東亜戦争についての日本バッシングを止めた方が良いと思う理由です。
　何より真実の日本はアメリカ人が考えている様な悪の帝国ではありませんでした。そして、大東亜戦争当時のアメリカ自体も、

Epilogue

アメリカ人が信じている様な道徳的な国ではありませんでした。アメリカ人はもうこの辺で歴史の真実に目を開くべきです。

　アメリカの将来の為に、日本との親善と協力が絶対必要です。そして、日本との親善を守る為に、アメリカ人は日本人の理解にもっと努力するべきです。そして両国は真の友人となって21世紀の世界をリードすべきです。

I must thank my publisher, Sakura no Hana, for asking me to do this book. It is a great chance for me to make a contribution to Japan, and I deeply appreciate it.

　さて、桜の花出版の皆様が、私にこの本を書く機会を下さった事を、とても感謝しています。

And to my manager and great friend, Mr. Uchino. He was always providing me with advice as to what should be included in this book. And he read through the whole Japanese text, proof reading it.

　それと、私のマネージャーで素晴らしい友人、内野さんに心から感謝します。彼は常にこの本の内容について相談にのってくれました。そして私が書いた日本語を全てチェックしてくれて、良いものが作れました。

And I must say thank you to my wife. Without her patience, advice, and help editing my Japanese text, this book would have been impossible.

　それから、私の妻にもお礼を言わなければなりません。彼女が私の日本語を根気よく修正してくれたり、相談にのってくれなければ、この本を書くことが出来ませんでした。

    I hope many Japanese people, and people of other nations, can find this book useful.

　私は、数多くの日本人に、そして他の国の人々にとって、この本が役に立つことを心から願っています。

September 15th, 2014
2014 年 9 月 15 日
Max von Schuler Kobayashi
マックス・フォン・シュラー小林

Max 小林

Fight for Japan!

■ Book List　参考文献

America encounters Japan
著者：William Louis Neumann
出版：Torchbooks

A very good account of the pre war years. It details the efforts of Christian missionaries to aid China and Christianize it, panic about Japan from Californians, and the efforts of the FDR administration to force Japan into starting war.

戦前の事を書いている良い本です。中国を日本から救うアメリカのキリスト教宣教師団の事、カリフォルニアでの日本人についてのパニック、フランクリン・D・ルーズベルト政権の日本が戦争を始める扇動について詳しく書かれています。

Soldiers of the Sun: The rise and fall of the Imperial Japanese Army
著者：Meiron Harries
出版：Random House

A history of the Japanese Imperial Army. The notation of only 17 military police at Nanking is on page 230.

日本帝国軍の歴史です。南京で憲兵が17人しかいなかったという事が230ページに書かれています。

Day of Deceit The truth about FDR and Pearl Harbor
著者：Robert Stinnett
出版：Touchstone

The FDR administration's 8 point plan to force Japan into starting war is on page 8. The book details how the FDR administration knew the attack on Pearl Harbor was coming.

フランクリン・D・ルーズベルト政権が日本に戦争を始めるように扇動した8つの計画を8ページに書いています。この本は、ルーズベルト政権が戦争開始前から真珠湾攻撃を知っていたという事を説明しています。

A great Aridness: Climate Change and the Future of the American Southwest
 著者：William deBuys
 出版：Oxford

Explains how the American southwest is turning into high desert that will be uninhabitable by the present population.

アメリカの南西部がまもなく深い砂漠になり、現在の人口が住み続ける事が不可能になる事を説明しています。

Embracing Defeat: Japan in the wake of WWII
 著者：John W. Dower
 出版：Norton

Explains how the Tokyo War Crimes Trials were extremely unfair, totally unjust.

東京裁判がとても不当で、不正義なものだったのかを説明しています。

War with out Mercy: Pacific War
 著者：John W. Dower
 出版：PANTEON BOOKS

Describes the propaganda efforts of Japan and the US in the war. Also mentions how US troops killed 50% of surrendering Japanese troops.

戦争中の日本とアメリカのプロパガンダについて説明しています。また、日本兵がアメリカ兵に降伏をした場合、半分が殺されたという事を説明しています。

What Soldiers Do: Sex and the American GI in France
 著者：Mary Louise Roberts
 出版：Chicago

Describes how American troops raped, pillaged and forcefully bought women for sex across France in WWII. Also mentions the American Comfort Women system in Hawaii in WWII.

第二次世界大戦でアメリカ兵がフランスの至る所で女性をレイプ、強盗、強制的に売春させていたかを説明しています。そして、アメリカ

のハワイの慰安婦システムについても書かれています。

This Kind of War
著者：T. R. Fehrenbach
出版：Macmillian

Describes the lack of morale and fighting ability of the US 2nd infantry division in the Korean war, when faced with difficulty. Also describes the collapse of American society among US POW's in Korea.

朝鮮戦争でのアメリカ第2歩兵師団の士気不足と、戦闘能力を説明しています。そして、朝鮮でのアメリカ捕虜の間でのアメリカ社会の崩壊について説明しています。

自滅するアメリカ帝国　日本よ、独立せよ
著者：伊藤貫
出版：文芸春秋

Provides an excellent description in Japanese of American exceptionalism.

〝アメリカ例外主義〟について日本語で優れた説明をしています。

A Republic, Not an Empire: Reclaiming America's Destiny
著者：**Patrick J. Buchanan**
出版：**Regnery Publishing,inc.**

He well describes the extensive compromises offered by Prime minister Konoye, such as withdrawal from Indo China and the bulk of China. The Japanese wish was that then America would lift the economic embargo. Yet Secretary of State Cordel Hull refused this, he felt that it was not enough. Truly, the Roosevelt administration wanted war.

近衛文麿総理大臣からの対米戦争回避の為の妥協の申し出を説明しています。例えば、インドシナと中国から撤退する事等です。日本の要求はアメリカが経済制裁を解除する事でした。しかしアメリカ国務長官コーデル・ハル氏がこの妥協案は十分ではないと拒否しました。やはりルーズベルト政権は開戦を望んでいました。

James Howard Kunstler

His website, written weekly, describes American financial and oil collapse.

彼のサイトでは、毎週アメリカの経済、石油がまもなく崩壊するという事を書いています。

・**The Guardian**
・**The Independent**
・**Rolling Stone**

These three news organizations all have published many articles concerning how US troops in Iraq and Afghanistan have killed and raped.

この三つのニュース機関は、イラク・アフガンでのアメリカ兵が好き勝手に人を殺したり、レイプをしたり、という事を公表する記事を沢山掲載しています。

John Toland

All of his works on WWII are illuminating. They provide a sympathetic view of Japan's war effort.

彼の第2次世界大戦の作品は全て良いものです。彼は日本の戦争に同情的な見方をしています。

マックス・フォン・シュラー 小林
(Max von Schuler‐Kobayashi)
牧師。歴史研究家。
1956年2月22日生まれ。父はドイツ系、母はスウェーデン系のアメリカ人。1974年岩国基地に米軍海兵隊として来日。その後、日本、韓国で活動。退役後、国際基督教大学で政治学を学ぶ。役者、コメンテーターとしても日本で活動。
「日出処から」代表講師。
2013年4月、全米で初めて慰安婦像を建立しようとしていたカリフォルニア州グレンデール市の市長と市議に宛て異議を唱えた手紙は動画にもなり、多くの人に支持されている。

アメリカ人の本音 THE TRUTH ABOUT AMERICANS

2014年10月18日　初版第1刷発行
2016年 3月 5日　初版第2刷発行

著　者　マックス・フォン・シュラー

発行者　山口　春嶽

発行所　桜の花出版株式会社
　　　　〒194-0021　東京都町田市中町 1-12-16-401
　　　　電話 042-785-4442

発売元　株式会社星雲社
　　　　〒112-0002　東京都文京区大塚 3-21-10
　　　　電話 03-3947-1021

印刷製本　モリモト印刷株式会社

本書の内容の一部あるいは全部を無断で複写（コピー）することは、著作権上認められている場合を除き、禁じられています。
万一、落丁、乱丁本がありましたらお取り替え致します。

© Max von Schuler 2014, Printed in Japan
ISBN978-4-434-19835-9 C0098

桜の花出版　話題の本

俳画集
行く道に花の咲かない道はなく

鮫島 芳子 著　　定価（1,300円＋税）

辛い時も悲しい時も、一人絶望に立ち尽くす時も、足下の花々は、あなたに生きる力を与えてくれる

最愛の息子を交通事故で失い、壮絶な悲しみに立ち向かうことになった著者に、息子のクラスメイトたちからの断えることのない花束が贈られる。その彼らの姿と、玄関の外にまで溢れる花々たちに著者は次第に癒されて、いつしか花々の絵と心の内を俳句に描き溜めるようになった。

そして、数年後、今度は最愛の夫を亡くし、体調を崩し、再びに絶望の縁に立たされる…。そんな著者を励ましてくれたのは、やはり、野にひっそりと咲く可憐で美しい花々だった。いつしか自然と俳句が出てくるようになり、書き溜めた絵と俳句を1冊の本にまとめたのがこの俳画集である。素朴な温かさが読む人の心に染み渡り、不思議と疲れた心を癒してくれる。自分のために、あるいは、周りの人のために、持っているととても心が温まる1冊。

人生の転機〈新装版〉　桜の花出版編集部

定価（890円＋税）

誰しもに必ず訪れる人生のターニングポイント

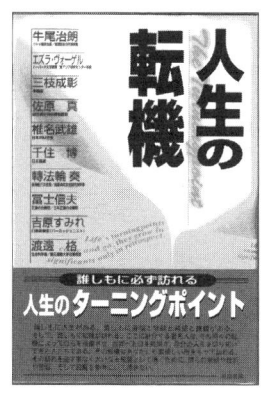

あなたの人生の岐路で、苦悩の中で、次なる飛躍の力となる言葉が、勇気と希望を与えてくれる。

その時々の転機によって自らを飛躍させ、世界へと目を見開き、自分の人生を切り開いた著名人の人生を紹介する。

転機は思いがけなく訪れる。どうやらそれは、人との出逢いと大きく関わりがあるようだ。運とは、人と人の間で生きている生き物なのかもしれない。それぞれの人生の軌跡は、転機は、自分から生み出すものだ、と訴えているような気がしてならない。読者各位がご自分や子どもや、周りの人生を考える上で、本書は大事な決断を伝えてくれるに違いない。

桜の花出版　話題の本

シリーズ日本人の誇り 10

朝鮮総督府官吏 最後の証言

筆者は、インタビュー時（平成２６年）９９歳。80年前の朝鮮で朝鮮人の知事が統括する行政組織で働き、朝鮮人と共に汗を流して働き、朝鮮は第二の故郷となった。その西川氏が証言する「日本人と朝鮮人はとても仲が良かった！」

<本書の取材記より>

日韓併合の実態を行政側から解説できる朝鮮總督府官吏としての証言はおそらく西川氏が最後であろう。

他に朝鮮で生活した方がいたとしても終戦時は幼少であったり、当時を知る家族から伝え聞いた話が殆どになる筈である。それは一つの貴重な体験ではあるが、「朝鮮總督府の施政がどういうものであったか」という視点で語ることは難しい。だからこそ、この元官吏である西川氏の証言及びその写真、資料は日韓併合時の実態を知る上で貴重な記録である。

ここに証言されている内容は、戦後教育を受けた人にとっては、驚きであるに違いない。

取材に於いて西川氏は、朝鮮のごく平穏な生活と日常に触れ、そこで語られるのは幸せな朝鮮人と日本人の姿であった。特に地方行政府は朝鮮人官吏が主体の組織であり、官や軍による売春婦の強制連行などあり得ないこと、不可能なことが繰り返し述べられている。

また、貴重な写真からも朝鮮人と日本人が普通に仲が良かったことが分かる。朝鮮人が日本人の上司になることも普通であり、職場の仲間と日朝合同の野球チームを作り他のチームと戦ったり、時に桜の下で酒を酌み交わした楽しい想い出も多く、朝鮮人と日本人は共に朝鮮の発展を願い職務に精励していたという。

まるで現代社会と変わらないような錯覚を覚えるが、正にこれが歴史の真実である。

B6判並製／定価（1,400円＋税）

桜の花出版　話題の本

RandomYOKO の 新・愛国論　YOKO 著

四六判並製／定価（1,360円+税）

こよなく日本を愛する超人気ブロガー Yoko（初代 YouTube NextUp 受賞者）が、日本の政治や歴史などについて明瞭な語り口で論理の矛盾を鋭く突く。

本書〈はじめに〉より

福岡出身のアーティスト、ビデオブロガーです。私は主に、YouTube の randomyoko2 というチャンネルとニコニコ動画を使って、政治や歴史について発信しています。音楽関連の動画は YouTube の randomyoko というチャンネルに投稿しています。

歴史の事実を歌った自作の投稿動画「韓国人慰安婦の歌」「韓国併合の歌」「靖国の歌」の反響は大きく、再生回数は１００万回近く（２０１４年６月末現在）になり、韓国のマスコミでも紹介されました。

今回動画やSNSでは伝えきれなかった思いや私の考えを、本という形でお届けすることになりました。私がこの本で言いたいことは単純です。私が日本を大好きだということ、そして、日本人はもっと素直に日本を好きになって、世界中に日本の素晴らしさを主張して欲しいということです。日本を好きだという気持ち、その日本を守りたいという当たり前の気持ちが愛国心だと思います。愛国という言葉に、故意に否定的なニュアンスを絡めたがる人達もいますが、自分の祖国や故郷を愛するのは自然なことです。世界中どの国でも、それが常識なのです。日本だけが自虐史観に毒されて、愛国心を口にすることが悪い事のように言われているのです。もう自虐史観からはいい加減覚醒しましょう。新しい時代の『新・愛国論』とでも呼ぶべきものを皆さんと共有できたら嬉しいと思います。

YOKO 初の本『新・愛国論』には知っておきたい日本の歴史・文化の知識や韓国への反論ポイントが満載。世界へ発信するための英語のフレーズやオリジナル曲『韓国併合の歌』の歌詞・楽譜も掲載！　若きリーダーの登場である！

桜の花出版　話題の本

『THE NEW KOREA　朝鮮(コリア)が劇的に豊かになった時代(とき)』
アレン・アイルランド著　桜の花出版編集部編　日英対訳

A5判並製／定価（2,800円＋税）

■植民地研究の第一人者アレン・アイルランドが日韓併合の業績を分析した決定版

著者は1901年、極東に3年間派遣され、英国、フランス、オランダ、日本による植民地経営のシステムを研究。6カ月間のフィリピン滞在の後、新しく設立されたシカゴ大学の植民地・商業学部の責任者に就任。その研究は、様々な客観的データを用い中立的で、学術的に高い評価を受けている。本書は、朝鮮の人口、鉄道、道路、郵便、電話、医療、公衆衛生、社会福祉、経済発展（様々な産業や貿易）等あらゆる観点から統計に基づき、日韓併合後の朝鮮の発展を分析し、日本統治を高く評価している。

『１９０７』 IN KOREA WITH MARQUIS ITO
ジョージ・トランブル・ラッド著　桜の花出版編集部編　日英対訳

A5判並製／定価（2,270円＋税）

■日本が朝鮮併合に到った経緯と伊藤博文の目指したものが分かる貴重な資料

米国心理学会の第2代会長であるイェール大学教授の著者が、伊藤博文初代統監と共に1907年、日韓併合前の朝鮮を訪問し、当時の実情をありありと記録した貴重な一次資料。2年後の1909年、伊藤博文が暗殺され、日韓併合へと時代は急展開していく。本書は、日韓併合の直前の朝鮮の実情や伊藤統監の情熱と苦悩を、ドキュメンタリー映画のように、生々しく伝えている。また、朝鮮での覇権を巡り飛び交う流言飛語についても、現地ならではの緻密な検証を行なっている。

『朝鮮はなぜ独立できなかったのか』
1919年朝鮮人を愛した米宣教師の記録　アーサー・J・ブラウン著　桜の花出版編集部訳

A5判並製／定価（4,400円＋税）

■朝鮮とそれを取り巻く世界情勢が詳細に理解できる最適の書

1900年代初頭のアジア情勢を分析した書で、828頁の大作。同じく朝鮮王朝末期の朝鮮を訪れた記録であるイザベラ・バード著『朝鮮紀行』より圧倒的に情報量が多いながらも紀行文のように読み易く、当時の様子を客観的に知るのに最高のテキストである。本書で触れられている内容は、朝鮮の国土や人々、朝鮮を巡るロシア・中国・日本の争い、極東の脅威としての日本、日本統治の有益性ほか、世界における日露戦争勝利の意義も鋭く分析。